LAND
OF MANY
HANDS

Women in the
American West

LAND OF MANY HANDS

Women in the American West

Harriet Sigerman

Oxford University Press
New York • Oxford

In loving memory of my mother,
Lillian Sophie Sigerman,
a proud daughter of Texas

Oxford University Press

Oxford   New York
Athens Auckland Bangkok Bogotá Bombay
Buenos Aires Calcutta Cape Town Dar es Salaam Delhi
Florence Hong Kong Istanbul Karachi
Kuala Lumpur Madras Madrid Melbourne
Mexico City Nairobi Paris Singapore
Taipei Tokyo Toronto Warsaw
and associated companies in
Berlin   Ibadan

Design: Greg Wozney
Picture research: Lisa Kirchner

Library of Congress Cataloging-in-Publication Data
Sigerman, Harriet.
Land of many hands : women in the American West / Harriet Sigerman.
p.   cm.
Includes bibliographical references and index.
Summary: A history of women's roles in the migration to and
settling of the American West.
ISBN 0-19-509942-7
1. Women pioneers—West (U.S.)—History—Juvenile literature.
2. Frontier and pioneer life—West (U.S.)—Juvenile literature.
3. West (U.S.)—History—Juvenile literature.
4. Overland journeys to the Pacific—Juvenile literature.
[1. Women pioneers. 2. Pioneers. 3. Frontier and pioneer life—West (U.S.)
4. West (U.S.)—History.] I. Title.
F596.S515   1997
978—dc21   97-30004
                   CIP

9 8 7 6 5 4 3 2 1

Printed in the United States of America
on acid-free paper

On the cover: *Sunrise, North Rim Grand Canyon.* Mabel Fraser, 1928.
Frontispiece: *Violet Bailey of Sutton, North Dakota*

C O N T E N T S

INTRODUCTION 7

CHAPTER 1
"The Land of My Forefathers":
Native Peoples and Early Hispanic Settlement 17

CHAPTER 2
"We Are Not Alone on These Bare Plains":
The Mosaic of Westward Migration 43

CHAPTER 3
"You Will Wonder How I Can Bear It":
Life on the Overland Trail 71

CHAPTER 4
"She Was a Neat and Efficient Housewife":
Homemaking on the Frontier 93

CHAPTER 5
"I Was Full of My Duties and My Pleasures":
Making a Life on the Frontier 113

CHAPTER 6
"I Love to Work with Cattle":
Western Women at Work 129

CHAPTER 7
"There Was a Spirit of Helpfulness":
Building New Communities 155

FURTHER READING 179

INDEX 186

INTRODUCTION

n March 1848, Abigail Malick of Tazewell County, Illinois, set out with her husband, George, and six children for the Oregon Territory. Rumors abounded that the U.S. government would give 640 acres to families who settled the new region. And, indeed, in 1850 Congress passed the Donation Land Act, which granted 640 acres to a settler and his wife after they had lived on and farmed the land for four years. The promise of free farmland beckoned the Malicks and thousands of others to the Pacific Northwest, a region with an abundance of natural resources and fertile land. For these homesteaders, the prospect of land ownership meant better economic opportunities, an escape from harsh eastern winters, or simply a chance to try a new way of life.

Like other travelers, the Malicks endured a six-month, 1,800-mile journey by covered wagon over muddy paths, treacherous mountain passes, and dangerous river crossings. They crossed a land that was poorly marked, with few roads, and no towns along the way where they could replenish their supplies. Only a few U.S. military forts connected them with their fellow citizens. To make matters worse, Abigail Malick reluctantly left behind a married daughter and three grandchildren.

Once the day's journey was done, settlers heading West used their nights to prepare for the next day's grueling journey.

The Malicks were well-prepared travelers who knew how to anticipate hazards along the way. But when Hiram, their strapping 17-year-old son, went swimming in the Platte River during a stopover in Nebraska Territory on a warm, sunny day, they were helpless to prevent the tragedy that followed. As his friends watched, horrified, Hiram struggled to stay afloat in the swirling river current, which was swollen from heavy April showers. Seven times he resurfaced and tried to swim his way to shore, but he was finally overcome by the surging river waters. "It has Almost kild Me," Abigail wrote much later, "but I have to bear it."

After grieving for Hiram, the Malicks settled into a relatively calm, prosperous life on their new farm near the Columbia River—only to lose their oldest son, Charles, two years later. Charles died under mysterious circumstances during an expedition to search for gold in California. The Malicks never learned the exact cause of his death, only various rumors—that he was robbed and died from his injuries, or was taken ill. After this fresh loss, Abigail woefully wrote, "trouble attendes me. Trouble trouble trouble. O lord when will it be over?"

But it wasn't over for her yet. Four years later, in the autumn of 1854, Abigail's husband died suddenly from a stroke, leaving Abigail alone to run their farm. Her children were little help. Abigail complained that Shin, her youngest son, gambled and would not lift a finger around the farm. "[Shin] Makes Me the Most trouble [and] whare he Aught to be A Comfourt to Me he is a trouble." One daughter died in childbirth, and another endured a difficult marriage before going insane.

Yet even as Abigail Malick bemoaned her family problems and the hard work of running the farm, it became the one satisfying constant in her life. "I have Abutiful teem of Creem colored Horses," she wrote her daughter back in Illinois. "One Is a Horse And the other Is A Mare. And I Have A most butiful Wagon and Butiful Harnice and A good plow and Harrow." With each passing year, Abigail made additional improvements to her land. She managed to find reasons not to return to

Illinois and left her claim only briefly during a violent clash between settlers and nearby Indian tribes.

The farm thrived. In her later years, Abigail was especially proud of the orchard she had planted—pear and plum trees "and peaches and Cheryes of difrent kindes and Chois Appoles Sutch As I Never Saw Eny In the States," she boasted. Abigail Malick's children proved to be a constant source of heartbreak for her, but her farm brought her a glowing sense of pride and security.

Abigail Malick's story echoes the experiences of thousands of other settlers who went west in search of better opportunities and who, facing hardship and tragedy, managed to wrest a bountiful life from the land. Settlers had been pushing back the western boundaries of the United States since the earliest days of the Republic. But starting in the 1840s, the region extending from the Mississippi River to the Pacific Ocean and from the Gulf of Mexico north to the border of Canada witnessed a historic land rush that brought fortune-hunters, settlers eager to build new communities, and adventurers seeking new ways to live.

The vast tracts of land available in the West enticed hundreds of thousands of people to undertake the long, difficult journey to stake their claim.

From 1841 to 1866, the heaviest years of migration, about 350,000 settlers journeyed west, most by land, some by ocean passage. Hundreds of thousands more traveled west during the remainder of the 19th century and well into the first two decades of the 20th century. Most settlers came from towns and cities in the eastern half of the United States, traveling west on the Overland Trail—the path that wagon trains followed from starting points along the Missouri River. But many

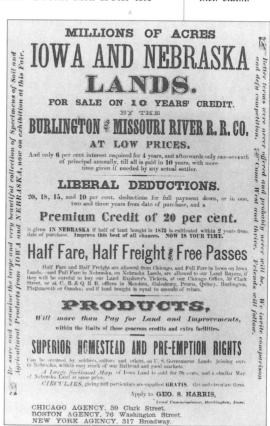

immigrants journeyed from faraway homes in Europe and Asia. They came by ship to New York City; Boston; Philadelphia; Chicago; Galveston, Texas; San Francisco; and other ports of entry, and then traveled to their western destinations by wagon or train.

By the mid-19th century, the West was the most ethnically diverse region of the United States, a mosaic of people from across the globe. From 1860 to 1900, between one-third and one-fourth of the western population had been born in another country. Women were a major part of this mosaic: Indian, Hispanic, white, African-American, and Asian and European immigrant women all played a vital role in the settlement, and also the despoilment, of the West. Native American women had long lived in the West, as members of ancient, diverse, and complex Indian cultures. Hispanic women, whose ancestors had come north from Mexico starting in the 16th century, were also part of a rich and highly developed cultural tradition. Other women came west from across the United States or from countries in Europe and Asia. They came as homesteaders and teachers, artists and journalists, prostitutes and outlaws, physicians and activists, domestics and nursemaids, and a myriad of other occupations. They came as free women and as slaves, as helpmates to their husbands, and as single women in search of a vocation. And wherever they settled, they left an indelible mark on the land and on the nation's destiny.

The westering experience, in turn, left an indelible stamp on women, presenting both challenges and opportunities. Women's experiences, and their impact on the land, varied according to their ethnic and cultural origins and their economic status. Some women endured many more hardships than others. Some were sadly defeated by their hardships, but many others rose to the challenges of helping to settle a new land.

In the 19th century, most white, middle- and upper-class Americans believed that a woman's highest duty was to marry, raise children, and create a virtuous home for her family. They believed that the grubby world of business and politics was too coarse for women's essentially pure nature—and many also believed that women lacked the intellectual skills and physical stamina to participate in political and economic affairs. Women could not vote, attend most colleges and universities, or enter the professions of law and medicine.

When the first wagon trains hit the dusty trails, many settlers carried these ideas about women with them. Westering men and women alike were unprepared for the hardships that lay ahead: the dirty, cramped quarters of a rolling wagon, the inadequate provisions for cooking tasty, nutritious meals, the dangerous river crossings and mountain passes, and the wild and rugged land they were traversing. These hardships and crude conditions undermined women's ability to fulfill their traditional social roles as wives and mothers, and often took an enormous toll on their health and well-being.

But other women exhilarated in the adventure and used these same hardships to break free from the social restraints governing their behavior. They found new strength and power in doing such "unladylike" tasks as driving oxen, roping cattle, cooking outdoors, and performing other demanding physical chores. And when they reached their new home, they marshaled the resources and learned the skills necessary to make a home in isolated wilderness shacks or in crude young western settlements. They managed to overcome the hardships of homesteading and, like Abigail Malick, felt an enduring attachment to the land.

Immigrant women from Europe and Asia faced unique challenges: not only did they confront the physical hardships of life on the frontier but they struggled to learn a foreign language—English—and foreign ways, often in the face of discrimination and hatred. Although they came to America for better economic opportunities or to flee from despotic governments, their new country did not welcome them; many native-born Americans did not want them to live or work in their communities. Immigrants were forced to live under the most meager conditions and take the least desirable or most dangerous jobs out West. Under these trying conditions, women of the western mosaic valiantly struggled to eke out a living and to keep alive their native customs and traditions.

Westerners of African and Mexican descent had even fewer opportunities and less freedom. In most areas, they were despised by their white neighbors and shunned by the community. Laws prevented them from living where they wished, exercising legal rights that other settlers had, obtaining an education, or using public transportation or recreation.

But the western experience was hardest for those who had been there the longest: Indians whose ancestors had settled the West long before Europeans arrived on the continent. To advance the new western settlement, the U.S. government drove Indians out of their homelands and sought to dismantle their religious, cultural, and economic traditions.

The westward movement took place during a time in which great struggles were being fought over the rights of women and ethnic minorities in American society. As the United States waged war for western lands against Mexico and the Indian nations, women were petitioning for the right to vote, Native Americans were fighting to hold onto their homelands, and African Americans were struggling to end slavery. In 1848, the United States expanded its borders after defeating Mexico in the Mexican-American War. The U.S. received as the spoils of war all of what is now California, Nevada, Utah, most of Arizona, and part of Colorado and New Mexico.

Also in 1848, around the time that gold was discovered in California, a handful of women in the tiny hamlet of Seneca Falls, New York, launched an organized movement to obtain the right to vote, seek work in professions that barred them because of their sex, such as law and medicine, and secure other economic and social rights, such as the right to own property and keep their wages after they were married and to sue for divorce.

Western women were in the forefront of the struggle to expand women's rights. Even before the passage of the 19th Amendment to the U.S. Constitution in 1920, which granted women the right to vote, women in most western states and territories had fought for and won that right. Throughout the West, women found work not only as teachers, nurses, boardinghouse keepers, and waitresses—all traditional forms of paid

work for women—but also as newspaper reporters and editors, cowgirls, land speculators, and doctors. And while their sisters in the East struggled to expand their power and visibility in their communities, western women were helping to build new communities—from raising money to construct buildings for schools and churches to creating religious and cultural organizations to bring a spirit of piety and fellowship to their new settlements.

From 1861 to 1865, the Civil War ripped the nation apart over the long-seething question of slavery. Like a prairie fire on the horizon, the threat of war darkened settlers' lives out West as they, too, hotly debated the future of slavery. Violent skirmishes over slavery in Kansas and in other western territories preceded the Civil War. During the war such western states as

A postmistress stands outside of the post office she ran in Cronin, Washington. The wide-open spaces of the West offered women many new and different kinds of work opportunities.

Missouri, Tennessee, Arkansas, and Texas witnessed fierce and bloody battles.

Throughout the 19th century, another war also raged—a war against the first inhabitants of the West, Native Americans. When the wagon trains reached their destinations in the West, they did not enter a land devoid of people or settlement. Instead, they encountered an array of highly developed Indian cultures that had lived throughout the West for thousands of years. But settlers' growing demands for the rich farming and mining lands of the West, and a belief in what some Americans called "manifest destiny"—the steady, inevitable expansion of the nation's borders all the way to Pacific shores—led to savage violence against Native Americans.

The course of westward migration is inextricably bound with this shameful history of government deceit, repression, and violence against American Indians. Within this web of deceit and violence, Indian women, who had long played a vital role in the social, economic, and religious life of their people, struggled to keep their families and communities intact as more settlers came.

But, backed by the power of the U.S. government, western settlers simply snatched the farming, hunting, and sacred burial grounds of Indian tribes. Before and after the Civil War, the U.S. military opened land for settlement by removing Indian tribes who had lived on that land for centuries and resettling them elsewhere. After the war, the government established a network of reservations. On these patches of land, thousands of Indians struggled to live and farm, and to keep alive cultural traditions that government officials tried to stamp out. When Indians resisted, they met the full and violent force of American military power. In California alone during the 1850s, the Indian population dropped from about 150,000 to about 30,000. Disease, starvation, U.S. military force, and a declining birthrate for Native Americans—all conditions brought on by a massive influx of gold seekers and others—accounted for this dramatic decline.

Against this backdrop of war and political and social strife, the wagons continued to roll west, the shiploads of passengers streamed into western ports, and the iron horse—the trains—bounded across the country, ferrying more travelers to western land claims. The westward movement was like a vast stage on which native peoples and settlers played out a dramatic struggle to survive and to carve out a hardy way of life on the land. In an often harsh and unyielding, but also bountiful land, western women did their part. They helped to keep their families fed, clothed, and sheltered; found new forms of paid work; struggled to preserve traditional customs and values; organized communities; and worked to expand their social and political rights. The dramatic story of westward expansion is also the story of the women—Indian, Hispanic, white, African-American, European, and Asian—who helped to settle the West and shape the course of American history.

CHAPTER 1

"THE LAND OF MY FOREFATHERS"

NATIVE PEOPLES AND EARLY HISPANIC SETTLEMENT

The first toilers on the land were native peoples who came to North America by foot, crossing over from what is now Russia to Alaska and across North America. They built communities throughout the Americas and developed their own languages and cultures. Their histories are not completely known, but some of their stories survive. As they huddled around campfires on bitterly cold winter nights, seeking the warmth and comfort of the crackling flames, or planted and harvested their crops, the elder members instructed the young people about the origins of their people, and about the beauty and power of the natural world.

The Acoma Pueblo people of what is now western New Mexico tell an ancient story of creation, migration, and cultural identity that goes back at least a thousand years. In this creation story, a spirit named Tsichtinako encountered two sisters, Iatiku and Nautsiti, who lived underground. Following the spirit's instructions, the sisters planted four kinds of pine trees underground. One of the pine trees grew faster than the others and made a small hole in the earth above, and the two sisters came up into the world aboveground.

Navajo women in Arizona weave blankets and spin yarn. Indian women's craftwork provided useful as well as ornamental objects for their communities.

The two sisters created the mountains, plains, canyons, and mesas that make up the Acomas' homeland. They grew plants and created animals. One of the sisters, Iatiku, gave birth to many children. Each child's name represented a different Acoma clan. Iatiku also gave life to the spirits of the different seasons and to the kachinas—the spirits who showed Iatiku's descendants how to be brave, live virtuously, and grow corn. After creating the kachinas, Iatiku then showed her people how to build their homes and villages, including the kiva, the sacred room in the village. The ceiling of the kiva represented the Milky Way and its walls the sky. As they worshiped inside the kiva, the Acoma people renewed their link to the earth and the sky.

The Acomas' story of their origins is only one of many creation stories told by native peoples. As new cultures developed, so did new creation stories. These stories, passed down from one generation to another, explained the origins and significance of each culture's deities, customs, and rituals.

Throughout what is now the continental United States, a wide variety of native cultures gradually developed, each with its own language, customs, and social and economic structures. The western regions were dominated by the Sioux, the biggest and most powerful of the western tribes, who inhabited the woodlands of Minnesota and the Great Plains. The Cheyennes lived in the country of Wyoming and Montana. Farther south, other Cheyenne tribes established villages on the Colorado and Kansas plains. The Apaches occupied the arid southwest region of Texas and New Mexico, and the Pueblos also lived in New Mexico. The Nez Percés settled the Blue Mountains of Oregon and the Bitterroot Range of the Rocky Mountains. Many smaller tribes also inhabited the western lands.

Although customs and traditions differed from one culture to another, at every stage of life they performed their duties against the backdrop of long-hallowed beliefs about the world and their place in it. Men mostly held more visible positions of authority, but women bore essential responsibilities because they provided the practical needs of their people—they grew the food and made the clothing and tools from the big animals caught by their men.

Each tribe also showed allegiance to its community of birth. Though both men and women tried to improve their social and economic status, they did so within the constraints of community-sanctioned rites and traditions: They strove to improve themselves in ways that benefited their communities and upheld their cultures' most sacred traditions. Among the Indian tribes of the Plains—predominantly the Hidatsa, Mandan, and Arikara societies—the clan, a matrilineal family grouping organized around the mother's kin relations, bore responsibility for all of its members. Each clan took care of its orphaned and elderly and helped any of its ailing or needy members. When women were pregnant, other clan members cared for their children and household, and when young men returned from hunting buffalo, they were expected to share meat with elderly clan members who had no other means of obtaining it.

This community-oriented outlook shaped native people's responses to the natural world as well. They did not seek to

The Acoma Pueblo people lived in these intricately constructed pueblos in what is now New Mexico.

own land to increase their individual wealth or prestige. Nor did they hunt for pleasure or simply to show off their skills. To Native Americans, the natural world was suffused with divine spirits; every plant, fish, bird, tree, rock, mountain, and river embodied a spirit that commanded respect, gratitude, even reverence. Although Indians killed buffalo for meat and for the clothing and shelter provided by the buffalo's hide, and although they fished and planted crops for consumption, they did not take these vital resources for granted. In war, on a hunt, during planting time or a trading mission with other tribes, Indians—ever mindful of the spirits' generosity—prayed to their gods.

In the West, many Native American cultures believed that a feminine principle underlay all creation. Just as the Acoma Pueblo people traced their origins to the two sisters Iatiku and Nautsiti, so the Indian societies of the Plains attributed their origins to a female force. According to Mandan and Hidatsa religious beliefs, First Creator and Lone Man (also known as First Worker and One Man) created the land and the male animals. But they, in turn, were created by the grandmother mouse, and the earth itself was created by the grandmother toad. Old Woman Who Never Dies was a female deity who ruled over all vegetation and the cultivation of crops.

In a culture in which the feminine principle was such a vital force, women held a special and powerful position. They played a central role in village economic, social, and ceremonial affairs. Although men held many of the main leadership positions in most Native American societies, these societies were often organized along matrilineal lines: Children traced their descent through their mother's side of the family, and clans were organized around the mother. A woman continued to live in her mother's household all of her life, and if she married, her husband and children lived in that household as well— even though the husband acquired his family identity through his mother.

Besides her parents and grandparents, a girl's household usually included her mother's sisters, whom she addressed as "mother," and their children, who were her "sisters" and "brothers." Even as late as the end of the 19th century, property was passed down from mother to daughter. In 1873, Margarita, a well-known Indian woman in southern California, inherited land from her mother, who in turn had inherited the land from her grandmother. Pueblo Indian women of New Mexico owned the dwellings they built and plastered for their families. Among the many reforms that American women's rights advocates fought for throughout the 19th century was women's right to retain ownership of their property, a right that most Native American women had long possessed.

Indian men and women had distinctly different roles in village life, but their roles were equally important to the community's well-being. Pueblo women gathered, prepared, and preserved food, and cared for children and domesticated animals. They also built and plastered structures and created pottery. Men hunted and grew crops, including corn, beans, squash, and cotton. Plains Indian women planted and harvested crops while men hunted buffalo and other big game. Women also processed the buffalo hides and meat. In most tribes, men went to war, and women prayed for them. And both men and women performed special rites and ceremonies to increase their skills and power.

In various ways, Indian women exercised power in their communities. Iroquois women, who not only grew and processed the food but also distributed it in their villages, were able to prevent war expeditions by withholding dried corn and meat from their men. Among Cheyenne tribes, women held the position of chief occasionally and exerted leadership roles in governing councils. Later on, as settlers encroached upon their lands and attempted to reorganize native men's and women's lives according to the patterns of their

Caring for children was one of the most important tasks that Indian women performed. Indian parents cherished their children and diligently taught them the values and traditions of their culture.

own social order, women no longer participated in councils, but they continued to exert strong influence over their husbands who did.

Until the late 19th century, Indian women also joined men on war expeditions. A few Cheyenne women fought in battle, captured horses from other tribes, and counted coup—collecting the scalps of those they had defeated in battle. Some Blackfeet and Dakota women also participated in warfare. Dakota women who had distinguished themselves in battle earned the right to police other women in the campsite and to punish any who were unruly.

At festive trade fairs, the women of each tribe traded their crops in exchange for meat, hides, tools and utensils, pots, needles, colored cloth, and other goods offered by women from other tribes. These sociable fairs masked a sophisticated network of trade among tribes throughout the West and even Canada. To trade fairs on the Plains came Assiniboin and Cree tribes from Canada, who brought English-made guns and other manufactured goods, and the Sioux, Cheyenne, Arapaho, and Crow, who had obtained horses, mules, and manufactured goods from the Spanish conquerors in Mexico and from other tribes at trade fairs in the Southwest and the far West.

The real economic trade, therefore, was conducted by women, who also transacted most of the trade and barter with nearby settlers. In the 1850s, according to F. V. Hayden, a white visitor among the Plains tribes of the upper Missouri River Valley, women from these tribes traded between 500 and 800 bushels of corn each season at the fort of the American Fur Company. Hayden claimed that "this trade on the part of the Indians is carried on by the women, who bring the corn by panfuls and the squash in strings and receive in exchange knives, hoes, combs, beads, paint etc., also tobacco, ammunition and other useful articles for their husbands. In this way each family is supplied with all the smaller articles needed for a comfortable existence."

Besides their agricultural activities, arts and crafts were an important part of most Native American women's lives, bringing status and wealth to a woman and her family. Young girls learned the special craft skills of their mothers, such as beadwork, basketry, pottery, or quilling, ornamental work using porcupine or bird quills. Blackfeet women painted pictures of both war and hunting on their tepees to illustrate their husbands' activities.

A talented and industrious woman could enlarge her husband's fortune by her craftwork, which brought payment in articles of clothing, tools, or food. And because a man's social position depended upon his ability to give away goods in rites and ceremonies, his wife's contribution to his largesse was vital to his status and prestige. Just as warriors were honored for their skills in battle, women were honored for their craftwork. Men counted coup to display their warrior skills, and women added a mark or notch to their tools for every hide they tanned or every tepee cover they sewed.

Women were well paid for their craftwork. In Sioux society, an intricately decorated robe brought one horse in return. Among the Pawnee, a woman who designed a tepee received foodstuffs such as flour, sugar, coffee, and cloth. Cheyenne women who built lodges received a pair of moccasins, a robe and blanket, a wooden bowl, or some other object for their work. Other societies set their own standards of barter for craftwork.

Women's craftwork kept their communities clothed, sheltered, and decorated—and also served important ceremonial functions. In the Sioux, Pawnee, Arapaho, and Mandan societies, women constructed and designed tepees used on sacred occasions, tanned and decorated hide robes used in ceremonies, and made and decorated containers used in rituals. Tanning white buffalo hides, the most exalted part of the animal's body, also involved special ceremony. In Assiniboin society, the wives of chiefs tanned these hides. Cheyenne and Dakota societies held elaborate ceremonies to consecrate the white buffalo hide, and among the Cheyenne, middle-aged or older women with special tanning skills and spiritual powers performed the tanning after being prayed over and absolved from taboos. In Dakota society, the tanner had to be a woman who had never had sexual relations.

*Buffalo Bird
Woman, a member
of the Hidatsa tribe
born around 1839.*

Women did not freely share their craft skills with each
other. Instead, they maintained a shield of secrecy to protect
their valuable knowledge. Basketmakers and potters often
worked apart from the rest of the village to keep their techniques secret. As Buffalo Bird Woman, a Hidatsa woman born
about 1839 in what is now North Dakota, explained, "Basketmakers would not let others see how they worked, because if
another wanted to learn how to make baskets she should pay a
good price for being taught." Some quillers even believed that if
they did quillwork without following the proper techniques

they might go blind or worse. This secrecy prevented the uninformed from trying their hands at the craft—and preserved the elite status of skilled craftswomen, who protected their vocation by instilling these fears.

Whether they were planting crops, making pottery or baskets, tanning hides, or building lodges, Native American women blended spiritual and practical concerns. Plains women blessed each new earth lodge they constructed, conducted special rites before and after planting their fields, and performed other rites to observe the death of a loved one. Cheyenne and Dakota societies held elaborate ceremonies to consecrate the white buffalo hide, and among the Cheyenne middle-aged or older women with special tanning skills and spiritual powers performed the tanning.

Because men could give more time to the ceremonial aspects of their lives, their ceremonies were more demonstrative and also more numerous than women's. But women's rituals, like men's, provided comradeship and mutual support for facing the challenges of life. On the Plains, Indian women conducted ceremonial rites as members of their age-grade societies. Age-grade societies were groups composed of members of the same sex and approximately the same age. Members of age-grade societies together performed the prescribed rituals and tasks appropriate to their stage in life. Women's age-grade societies served three important purposes: to prevent loss of life in warfare and celebrate martial victories, ensure a bountiful crop and give thanks for the harvest, and bring about a successful buffalo hunt.

As they grew older, members of each age-grade society moved up the ladder into the next age-grade society. As a girl approached puberty, the women of her lodge, or house, taught her about how her body functioned. In Hidatsa culture, the earliest age-grade society for girls was the Skunk society, which performed dances after war victories. Young married Hidatsa women joined the River or Enemy societies. They participated in victory parades after warriors returned from successful war exploits. Between the ages of 30 and 40, Hidatsa women joined the Goose society. And after they were no longer of childbearing age, women moved up into the White Buffalo Cow society, the most prestigious age-grade society, which was responsible for calling the buffalo for the winter hunt. Age as well as appropriate behavior determined a member's advancement up the hierarchy.

One of the most important rituals that younger Plains women performed was "walking with the buffalo." Before the annual buffalo hunt, the younger married women had sexual intercourse with men who had excelled in hunting and war. They believed they were having sex with the buffalo, whom they regarded as a sacred god; they wished to appease him so that he would send herds of buffalo for their husbands to capture. Later, they had sexual relations with their husbands to transmit the older men's power and courage to them.

Indian women of the far western societies observed special rituals as well. Among the Pomo and Yurok societies of California, women often served as shamans. Pomo women performed ritual wailing and sang songs to ease childbirth and ward off illness when taboos were broken. Cupeno women in California sang "enemy songs," in which they told about groups within the village that were not abiding by the community's rules. As they sang, they rose up on their toes and danced in a special, jerking motion. Women also danced to personal songs that had been revealed in their dreams and visions.

Starting in childhood, women learned to perform these special tasks and rituals as well as their everyday duties. Young and old spent most of their waking hours together. Thus adults had plenty of opportunity to transmit the lessons of their culture to their children. Chona, a member of a Papago tribe in Arizona during the late 19th century, recalled waking up before dawn in wintertime to the sound of her father's low, gentle voice, imparting instructions to his children. "Open your ears," he said, "for I am telling you a good thing. Wake up and listen. You boys, you should go out and run. So you will be swift in time of war. You girls, you should grind the corn. So you will feed the men and they will fight the enemy. You should practice running. So, in time of war, you may save your lives." If Chona fell back asleep, her father would pinch her ear. "Wake up!" he demanded. "Do not be idle!"

Plains Indian children enjoyed carefree days of play until they turned seven or eight. At about age seven, girls began to help with such household tasks as gathering firewood. But even this could be a time for fun. Buffalo Bird Woman recalled: "On the return from the woods we walked in single file, our loads on our backs, my two mothers leading, talking and laughing and telling funny stories."

After a buffalo hunt, young girls carefully watched their mothers and grandmothers scrape clean the buffalo hides and tan them. They also helped their mothers decorate the hides; every girl had her own sewing kit that included awls for needles, sinew threads, paints, beads, and porcupine quills.

Then in the spring and summer, girls followed their mothers to the fields to learn how to plant and harvest. As they all worked together at harvest time, grandmothers recounted their village's history and traditions.

Corn, which could be eaten off the stalk, stored for the long winter, or ground into meal, was their most important crop—even more important than trees, which were cut down when their shade blocked the sun's rays from reaching the slender cornstalks. In Buffalo Bird Woman's tribe, the women built a platform on which girls and young women and even their female elders sat and sang as they watched over the corn. "We cared for our corn in those days as we would care for a child," Buffalo Bird Woman remembered. "For we Indian People loved our gardens, just as a mother loves her children; and we thought that our growing corn liked to hear us sing, just as children like to hear their mother sing to them."

In Arikara tribes, girls and their families observed a special ceremony to mark the onset of puberty. The girl's parents chose a highly respected elder man or woman to officiate, and inside a ceremonial structure she went before an altar. There her clothing was removed and she was dressed in a garment similar to a short skirt and painted all over with white clay. The elder addressed her, reminding her that she was no longer a child but a woman with responsibilities to her village. She was brushed down with a stalk of sweetgrass and dressed in new clothes. The sweetgrass symbolized positive spiritual influences and was an appeal to all of the good powers in the four quarters of the world to watch over and protect her. Her new clothing symbolized her rite of passage into womanhood. The elder prayed over her and urged her to be virtuous and loyal and to love and honor Mother Corn always.

The Yuroks, a California tribe, believed that women experienced their highest powers during their menstrual period and could not deplete their time and energy with mundane tasks. Instead, women spent the duration of their period in concentrated meditation to accumulate greater spiritual energy. They retreated to isolated huts, bathed in the river, and performed rituals to enhance their spiritual powers.

Marriage was the next milestone in a Native American woman's life. Plains Indian tribes practiced polygyny, in which a man was married to more than one woman. Usually a man married all of the sisters in one family. The practice of polygyny could be advantageous to both men and women. Co-wives shared the burdens of keeping house, and men prospered from the products of their wives' labor.

In some tribes, marriages were arranged by a couple's parents. Chona's parents, for instance, chose a mate for her, then lectured her on her duties as a wife: to be industrious and obedient to her husband and her husband's parents, and to refrain from gossiping. Sioux men chose their own wives, but only after they had distinguished themselves in battle. Young men and women of the Hidatsa tribe found ways to flirt with each other, and if both sets of parents approved of the match, then elaborate preparations for the courtship and ceremony began. These included the practice of bride-price, a ritual exchange of gifts between the bride and groom's families. The groom's family usually gave several horses to the bride's father and brothers. Upon accepting these gifts, which signaled their approval of the marriage, the bride's family gave gifts to the groom's family when the couple began to live together.

Childbirth was a special female-centered ritual. Among the Chilula of northern California, grandmothers, mothers, aunts, and sisters helped the pregnant mother by taking charge of her work duties for the last few weeks preceding childbirth. As labor approached, a medicine woman dug a shallow pit in the ground and filled it with warm coals, collected fir boughs to steam for purifying the mother, and brewed special teas to help her dream about animals that would protect and assist her, such as female deer, bears, and wolves. The medicine woman delivered the baby, and the mother's female relatives nursed her and helped care for the infant.

A Navajo woman looks after her grandchild. The elderly commanded great respect within their villages.

As women aged, they commanded greater respect and authority within their villages. In Plains tribes, women who had assisted at childbirth performed other medical duties for their village. In many ceremonies that younger women were barred from attending, they participated by helping to pass along traditions to young men. An elderly woman's children and grandchildren provided for her needs. If she had lost her children or had never borne children, her clan took care of her. As she prepared to die, she provided herself with the most beautiful buffalo robe she could make or arrange to have made, and as death approached, friends and relatives beseeched her to carry messages to their dead in the spirit world.

Immediately after a Plains Indian woman died, her family painted her body and dressed her in her special burial robe. Then they placed her body in hides tied with leather thongs and put the encased body on an outdoor scaffold, with her head positioned to the northwest and her feet to the southeast. Over a four-day period, relatives came to the scaffold to mourn. At the end of this official mourning period, a woman from her father's clan performed a special ritual to send her spirit away, and her relatives divided up her property. Her daughters inherited her lodge, fields, and household goods.

Across the sprawling West, scores of Indian societies lived for centuries in this manner, fiercely adhering to their hallowed beliefs and customs, synchronizing their lives and activities to the rhythms of the seasons, and transmitting their tribal traditions to the next generation.

As the first settlers trickled in, Native Americans both traded and battled with them. These first settlers were Spanish and, starting in the 16th century, they came up north from Mexico. In 1519, the Spanish soldier Hernán Cortés defeated the Aztec emperor Montezuma and seized Mexico, a land rich in gold and other natural resources. As Spanish conquerors interacted with their Mexican subjects, a new bloodline of people emerged called Hispanics. Eager to gain more riches, Spanish explorers made expeditions into the border regions that now divide the United States from Mexico to search for fabled riches and legendary wonders. In 1540, Francisco Vásquez de Coronado led an expedition through what is now Arizona and New Mexico, and in 1598, 130 Hispanic women and about 400 Hispanic men established the first permanent settlement in what is now New Mexico, then called New Spain.

While the men went on long expeditions to explore the region, the women cultivated and harvested fields of corn and other crops. The Hispanic settlers encountered mostly Pueblo Indians, and though they quickly gained control of the region by armed force, both cultures gradually learned from each other and adapted the other's cultural traditions to their own. Pueblo women, forced to work for their Hispanic conquerors, began preparing Hispanic foods and using Hispanic tools and livestock such as horses—an animal they had not seen before—in their daily tasks. They replaced cotton as the main

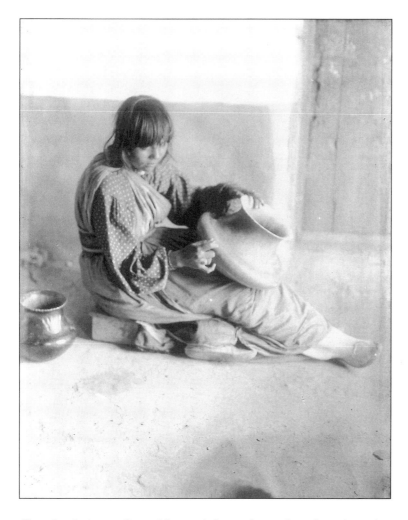

A Pueblo potter at work. Pottery, like other Indian crafts, required special skills and knowledge.

fiber in their textiles with wool from sheep that the Hispanics had brought.

In turn, the Hispanics admired the artistry of Pueblo women's pottery and relied on Pueblo women to build and repair their homes and churches. Pueblo women had long been expert plasterers who built and plastered their own adobes. Gradually, Hispanic women learned these skills and became the plasterers for Hispanic buildings. Hispanics also adapted other social and cultural practices of the Pueblos.

But under Spanish rule, the traditional Indian way of life and family, with its extended network of kin relations, suffered immeasurably. Pueblo women continued their traditional tasks, but they were also forced to labor for the Spanish *encomenderos,* or overlords. They toiled as domestics in Hispanics' homes, where they were subjected to sexual abuse by soldiers and other settlers, and were forced to produce food for the Hispanics as well as for their own families.

Hispanics forced their Indian subjects to renounce their religious traditions and convert to Catholicism, but the Pueblo Indians managed to practice their religious rituals secretly by conducting them in underground kivas, or ceremonial chambers. As the Spanish continued to gain control of other regions in the Southwest, other Indian populations suffered as well. In California alone, between 1769, when Hispanic settlement began there, and 1848, when gold was discovered and Anglo, or non-Hispanic white, settlers started flocking to the region, the Native American population dropped by 50 percent, from about 300,000 to 150,000. This dramatic decline, caused primarily by disease, was most pronounced where Indians labored for Hispanics—on Hispanic-owned ranchos and in missions established by Catholic priests.

Mission life was especially hard. Catholic priests founded missions to convert Indians to Catholicism and to further secure Spanish control in the Southwest. Protected by soldiers of the Spanish monarchy, Father Junípero Serra and the Spanish priests who served under him established nine missions along the California coast. They founded the first mission in San Diego in 1769 and, traveling on foot, worked their way up the coast to establish eight more. The path they traveled came to be known as El Camino Real. Other missionaries founded 14 more missions. The friars singled out Native American tribes for conversion to Christianity, and with the help of Spanish soldiers they gathered their subjects, often forcibly, into the mission compounds. By 1834, more than 7,000 Indians had been baptized at six northern California missions. Indian couples once joined in marriage by traditional Native American customs were remarried in the Catholic Church, and their infants were baptized as Catholics. These rites helped to weaken their link to their native cultures.

Indian labor was the backbone of mission life, and the products made at the missions, in turn, were the basis of California's economy under Spanish rule during the late 18th century. On the missions, Indian laborers built new buildings, herded cattle, planted crops, and produced goods for consumption at the missions or for export. They did whatever was necessary to keep the missions flourishing—often against their will.

Native American women especially felt the hardships of mission life. They were forced to give up many of their own ways and learn foreign customs. They learned how to make cheese and butter, harvest grapes and grain, weave, spin, and sew. At Mission San Diego, up to 50 or 60 women spun wool, flax, and cotton; wove yarn into cloth; threshed wheat; pounded bark for tanning; and hauled sand and cow manure for tile masons. They also ground wheat and learned how to make bread. To make matters worse, Spanish soldiers at the missions took sexual advantage of Native American women. From these soldiers, Indian women contracted venereal disease and other deadly diseases.

Some women resisted the missionaries' efforts to destroy their former way of life. Toypurina was a 24-year-old Gabrielina who urged the chiefs and warriors of six *rancherías,* or farm encampments, to rise up against the soldiers and friars at San Gabriel Mission in 1785. When she was arrested and interrogated before the royal governor, she defiantly declared,

As the Spanish gained control of the Southwest, they brought with them their religion, Roman Catholicism, and forcibly converted thousands of Indians.

"I hate the padres and all of you, for living here on my native soil, for trespassing upon the land of my forefathers and despoiling our tribal remains."

By 1848, when the United States defeated Mexico in the Mexican-American War and expanded its territorial boundaries, more than 75,000 Hispanics were living in the Southwest. Although they shared a common language, Spanish, a common religion, Catholicism, and common Spanish roots, Hispanic communities were highly diverse. Different dates of migration from Mexico and different settlement patterns, varying geographic conditions, and encounters with a variety of Indian populations created a rich diversity of customs and cultural practices in Hispanic settlements throughout the Southwest.

In their villages, Hispanic women, like Indian women in their own societies, played an important role. Although the Hispanic family was patriarchal—that is, the father or the oldest male commanded supreme authority and the women deferred to that authority—women could own or inherit their own property after they were married as well as share joint ownership of property with their husbands—long before Anglo women enjoyed such rights—and their daughters and sons usually inherited land equally, though daughters sometimes received livestock, furniture, and household goods instead of land. Hispanic women could initiate divorce proceedings, and they actively pursued business enterprises, bought or rented additional land, and defended their interests in court. The *alcade*, or Hispanic courts, often upheld their rights. Less wealthy Hispanic women baked, sewed, and served as herbal healers, or *curanderas,* to contribute to the family economy.

Unlike early settlers in the eastern United States, Hispanic men usually willed most of their property to their wives rather than to their children. As a result, a number of Hispanic women became major landowners after their husbands died. Among them was Doña Vicente Sepùlveda of California, a widow who managed her own ranch. Apparently, she was an astute businesswoman. Captain William Heath Davis recalled how he sold her between two to three thousand dollars worth of goods and, in turn, purchased several hundred dollars worth of brandy from her. "There was no haggling over price," he said. "She quietly named it."

But most Hispanic women were not so wealthy. Instead, they and their husbands owned a small lot, a house, and the land immediately surrounding it. The rest of the land and the sources of water were owned by the entire village. Villages pooled their labor as well. While the men plowed, hoed, harvested, and cared for the livestock, the women plastered houses and churches, baked bread, spun wool, and stuffed mattresses together. Plastering the walls of their homes and public buildings enabled women to work together to create an aesthetically pleasing village environment.

But among their most important tasks was maintaining their gardens, where they cultivated melons, chili peppers, onions, garlic, native tobacco, sweet corn, green beans, radishes, and pumpkins—all staples of their diet. They also cared for whatever livestock their families owned, such as goats and chickens, and made cheese and other dairy products. Their gardens—and the produce from them—gave Hispanic women an important social and economic role in their communities.

Both Hispanic men and women were expected to marry. Marriage was the individual's link to the community, and bearing children strengthened that link. Because children were important, the village midwife, who delivered them, was a key figure in the community. Both men and women villagers accorded her respect and treated her as a leader. Women confided in her, and new parents often chose her to be a godmother to the infants she delivered.

Into the patchwork of Hispanic and Indian cultures in the Southwest came Anglo settlers, first merchants and adventurers who started trickling into the region around the 1820s and later gold seekers and families. Many early Anglo male settlers married into the territory's elite Hispanic families, just as earlier Spanish conquistadors had married Mexican and Indian women or taken them as mistresses. As more black settlers—though never a huge number—ventured to the Southwest, they, too, married Hispanic women. Gradually, the region became a stage for the intermingling of people from a variety of ethnic backgrounds. But these encounters were marked not by cooperation but by mutual suspicion, disdain, resistance, and violence.

Growing Anglo settlement altered both Native American and Hispanic women's important roles within their own communities. As more Anglos arrived, they imposed their cultural values and business practices and snatched the most fertile lands from Indians and Hispanics. They imposed an economy based on money rather than on the exchange of goods. Gradually, they gained control over local economies, and the only way many Hispanic families could survive was by working as wage laborers for Anglos. Land that Hispanic women once cultivated now belonged to homesteaders, and women were forced to work for wages as seamstresses, cooks, laundresses, domestics, and prostitutes—with little control over their hours or conditions of work.

For example, the transformation of Los Angeles, California, from a Hispanic to an Anglo-dominated community reflects the disruption of traditional Hispanic life in the Southwest. In the early 19th century, Los Angeles was a leisurely, relaxed town in which Hispanic residents gathered in the plaza, attended *corridas* (bullfights), and enjoyed frequent *bailes* (dances). The town's Spanish architecture evoked the flavor of Hispanic life there. Wealthy women maintained houses on the plaza as well as haciendas, or large estates, on ranchos farther out from the town. By the 1850s, Los Angeles was under Anglo political control, but Hispanics still maintained their cultural traditions. By the 1860s, however, intermarriage between Hispanic women and Anglo men had increased and the children of these unions were inclined to adopt Anglo culture.

As older Hispanic residents lost their land and wealth to the Anglo newcomers, they were compelled to move into poorer districts, along with newly arriving immigrants from Sonora, Mexico. Only a minority of Californios, or native-born Californians of Hispanic origin, managed to hold on to their land and cultural traditions. By 1880, they were overwhelmed

The Ontivares clan was one of the few Californio families who managed to hold on to their land after California became a part of the United States.

by a still-growing and ever more powerful Anglo population. All Hispanics—native-born to California and immigrant— comprised only 15 percent of Los Angeles's population, and what was once a plaza-centered village became a barrio—a district reserved for poor, struggling Hispanics.

Hispanic women also lost certain legal rights. When California became a state in 1850, Hispanic women had to adhere to new state laws that gave their husbands control over their property. In 1860, the state legislature passed a new inheritance law, which affected all California citizens, including Hispanics: Upon a wife's death, property that once went to her children now went to her husband, leaving female children in particular dependent upon their fathers.

Many Hispanics feared that American settlers and soldiers would harm them. When Mexican troops left Tucson, Arizona, in 1853 after the U.S. purchased that portion of land from Mexico, many Hispanic residents fled with them. "It was rumored," said Doña Atanacía Santa Cruz, a Tucson resident, "that as they advanced the American troops were seizing all that had formerly belonged to Mexico, abusing and even killing families."

Even when they did not fear the Americans, Hispanics resented them for pushing them farther out and for taking the good farming and grazing land. They were also appalled by what they regarded as the Americans' crude manners and morals.

For their part, settlers were influenced by guidebooks that characterized Hispanics as "ignorant," "superstitious," and "barbarous." Anglo settlers were generally fearful and ill disposed toward their Hispanic neighbors. Mary Helm, who lived in Texas during the 1830s, described Hispanics as "weak, cowardly, and lazy [and] the very antithesis of the Anglo American." She dismissed Hispanics as "the debris of several inferior and degraded races." Helm, who lived in segregated surroundings, seldom came into contact with Hispanics.

To many Americans like Helm, all but the most elite Hispanic women were poor, dirty, immoral, and crude, and Hispanic men were lazy, filthy, stupid, cowardly, and thieving. Women who visited the grand ranchos and haciendas of California, Texas, and New Mexico were more favorably disposed toward Hispanics than those whose only exposure was to poor Hispanics. Anglo women of the 1850s and 1860s, many of them army wives who came into contact with Hispanics throughout the Southwest, were fascinated by Spanish customs and architecture. They attended fiestas and visited upper-class Hispanic homes, and some tried to learn Spanish and to master Spanish cooking. Anna McKee of Illinois was enthralled by Hispanic women's "elegant dresses—silks, satins, and velvets and what beauties some of the girls were." Margaret Hecox, who came to California in 1846, during the Mexican-American War, commented that far from being hostile "the Mexicans with whom we met treated us most kindly...particularly the Spanish women, who came to us as we traveled along...bringing us offers of homemade cheese, milk, and other appetizing food." She later learned Spanish and became close to her Mexican neighbors, "whom I learned to love like sisters." Still, some American women continued to harbor prejudices. Teresa Viele derided the lower-class Hispanics whom she encountered as "lazy," the priests a "dissolute, carnal, gambling, jolly set of wine bibbers," and the upper class as a "relic of the departed glories of their line."

If the growing Anglo presence in Hispanic-settled regions was disruptive, its impact on Native Americans was disastrous. Disease, starvation, and a declining birthrate for Native Americans—all conditions brought on by a massive influx of gold seekers and others—accounted for this catastrophic decline. Babies died of disease or starvation because their mothers did not have the nutrients to breast-feed them properly. Violence also claimed Indian lives. After Pomo Indians in California killed two particularly cruel Anglo ranchers in 1850, the U.S. cavalry massacred all the members of a Pomo fishing village at Clear Lake, in northern California.

In northern California as well, Hispanics and, later, Americans captured Native American children and sold them as indentured servants. Fear of kidnapping continued into the 20th century. Elsie Allen, a Pomo woman born in 1899 near Santa Rosa, California, recalled how her grandmother hid her when whites visited their isolated home.

As settlers advanced farther west throughout the 1850s and 1860s, Native American women found their important tribal roles gradually changing and diminishing, especially as their tribes lost control of the land. In 1822, American traders established a series of trade posts on the Plains, and Indians traded and sold more animal hides to Anglo traders. Indian women continued to clean and process the hides, and Indian men negotiated the transactions. As the demand for hides increased, women were forced to spend more time processing them— while still carrying out their many other domestic and agricultural duties. And as families and clan groups relied increasingly on the income from the trade in hides, the men who conducted this trade gained more social and economic power and women became more economically dependent upon them.

But women also found ways to contribute to the family economy. Plains Indian women continued to grow and harvest corn, and to sell this corn to traders. California Indian women sold the wild herbs and nuts they gathered, as well as their pottery and baskets, and worked as domestics on ranches.

White settlers indifferently encroached upon Native Americans' ancestral and farming lands, and wantonly destroyed the land and game that had sustained them. They also prompted the forced removal of Indians to other regions. In the 1830s, even before large numbers of settlers began to flock to the West, government troops forcibly removed 85,000 Indians of the Cherokee, Choctaw, Creek, Chickasaw, and Seminole nations from southeastern states to a territory reserved for them west of Arkansas. About 4,600 Cherokee perished on the infamous Trail of Tears, the route they were forced to cross under armed military guard in 1838. Starting in Georgia, where they were cruelly rounded up by soldiers armed with bayonets, they crossed on foot and in wagons, and also by boat, through blinding snow, ice, and winter storms. They were allowed to take only what they could carry on their backs and had to leave all other possessions behind, including their horses, cattle, and household effects. Rebecca Neugin, who was only a child when her family was rounded up, recalled how soldiers "drove us out of our house to join other prisoners in a stockade." After the soldiers took them away, her mother begged them to let her

Thousands of Cherokees died on the infamous Trail of Tears in 1838. Forced from their homes in Georgia, the Indians were marched, under brutal conditions, to a settlement in Oklahoma.

return and retrieve some bedding. "So they let her go back and she brought what bedding and a few cooking utensils she could carry and had to leave behind all of our other household possessions."

Even elderly women, frail and feeble, were forced to walk with heavy burdens on their backs. "Womens cry and make sad wails," recalled one Cherokee on that treacherous march. "Children cry and many men cry, and all look sad like when friends die, but they say nothing and just put heads down and keep on go towards West." Those who died along the way were hurriedly buried and the march continued, day after day, through wind and snow, until the exhausted Cherokees and their armed guards reached Oklahoma.

Both Native Americans and settlers engaged in bloody conflicts, and innocent people on both sides were massacred. As settlers advanced, claiming Indian tribal lands as their own and breaking the terms of treaties they had signed, Native Americans tried to defend their land. In the 1850s, Pacific Northwestern tribes rose up to defend their homes, and in New Mexico in 1861, Apaches killed 46 settlers and took several women and children captive. A year later, in Minnesota, the Sioux fought mightily against oncoming settlers, forcing the evacuation of the settlement of New Ulm. Cheyenne and Arapaho tribes in Colorado raided settlements to drive home-steaders away. In Apache tribes, some women joined their men on the battleground, while others served as messengers and emissaries between Apache warriors and U.S. military officers.

But these tragic clashes between Native Americans and settlers were a prelude for worse events to come. Armed con-flict, disease, famine, forced resettlement, and cultural subjuga-tion gradually destroyed the communal, agrarian way of life that Native Americans had known for centuries. Sarah Winnemucca, a member of the nomadic tribe of Piutes who lived in the deserts of northern Nevada, aptly described the advancement of settlers into her homeland: "They came like a lion, yes, like a roaring lion, and have continued so ever since, and I have never forgotten their first coming."

CHAPTER 2

"WE ARE NOT ALONE ON THESE BARE PLAINS"

THE MOSAIC OF WESTWARD MIGRATION

I n 1852, a popular camp song included these two lines: *Come along, come along—don't be alarmed, Uncle Sam is rich enough to give us all a farm.*

Later, in the territories of Colorado and New Mexico, pamphlets lured homesteaders west with these words: "Where to Go to Become Rich." Ever since the first colonists sailed across the Atlantic Ocean to America's shores, seeking religious freedom and the opportunity to build a new Promised Land, the open spaces of the North American continent have been equated with greater opportunity—with freedom to live as one pleased and with economic as well as spiritual enrichment.

The history of America, then, is the history of a nation on the move, as settlers continually pushed the boundaries back to seek new land and opportunity. In 1803, in perhaps the greatest land deal since the Dutch bought Manhattan island in 1623, President Thomas Jefferson purchased the Louisiana Territory sight unseen from France for $15 million. He then dispatched two explorers to survey what he had bought. The Louisiana Purchase extended the nation's boundaries west from the Mississippi River to the Rocky Mountains and north from the Gulf of Mexico to the border of Canada. It doubled the

This engraving, entitled Pilgrims on the Plains, *appeared in* Harper's Weekly *in 1869, at the height of the westward migration. Pictures such as this aroused people's curiosity and enthusiasm for the westering experience.*

nation's size and opened fertile new farmland and grasslands for settlement.

Starting in the early 19th century, homesteaders left the crowded towns and villages of the eastern seaboard and began to settle the trans-Appalachian West—the region that is now Michigan, Ohio, Indiana, Illinois, Kentucky, Tennessee, Mississippi, and Alabama.

By the 1830s, farmers and homesteaders had set their sights even farther west—to Minnesota, Iowa, Missouri, Arkansas, and Texas. One farmer from western Illinois complained that people were settling "right under his nose"— though his closest neighbor was 12 miles away. He moved his family to Missouri but, still not satisfied, packed them up yet again and pushed on to Oregon. A severe nationwide depression in 1837 had led to bank closings and drastic wage cuts, leading many people to explore economic opportunities outside the crowded cities. The annexation of the Republic of Texas in 1845 and the additional land that the United States acquired from Mexico after the bloody Mexican-American War also beckoned settlers west. Then, in 1848, the discovery of gold in California ignited the pioneer spirit as never before.

Whatever their destinations or their reasons for traveling, the pioneers shared the dream of a better life in the West. Peter Burnett told his wife that he was fed up with the Midwest and wanted to move to Oregon: "Winters it's frost and snow to freeze a body; summers the overflow from Old Muddy drowns half my acres; taxes take the yield of them that's left. What, say, Maw, it's God's country [in Oregon]."

The quest for better economic opportunities was the number one reason for going to "God's country." But some people went west with a more fundamental goal in mind—personal safety. Gardener Johnson, an enslaved African-American woman whose owner offered to set her free before he and his family went west, chose instead to go with them. She explained, "I was afraid to accept my liberty, much as I would have liked to stay [behind]. The word of a Negro was of no value in court.... Negroes were the same as cows or horses and were not supposed to have morals or souls. I was afraid to accept my liberty, so I came to Oregon with my owners."

But a woman didn't have to be enslaved to equate the West with a better way of life. In 1862, as the nation was engulfed in the Civil War, President Abraham Lincoln signed the Homestead Act. This law enabled "any person who is the head of a family, or who has arrived at the age of twenty-one years" and was or intended to become a U.S. citizen to file for a quarter section, or 160 acres, of free land. The Homestead Act enabled single, divorced, widowed, and other women who were heads of households to file claims in their own names. Older and younger single women, widows with and without children, divorced and deserted women, and even some married women who were considered the heads of their households because their husbands were ill or incapacitated became homesteaders.

The act required homesteaders to pay a $14 filing fee and granted them five years to improve, or prove up, their land. During these five years, the applicant could not change residency or abandon his or her claim for more than six consecutive months at any given time. Any applicant who did not meet these conditions lost all rights to the land. In 1912, Congress amended the act by lowering residency requirements from five to three years and permitting a longer absence each year for those who had jobs or family ties elsewhere. Within the general residency requirements, the actual amount of time a settler lived on her claim varied from a few days every once in a while to continuous residence. Other Congressional acts also encouraged both women and men to homestead. The Oregon Donation Land Law of 1850 allowed married women to claim a half section, or 320 acres, of land in their own right to supplement their husbands' land claims.

But the Homestead Act of 1862 was historic because for the first time in their nation's history all free American women, single, divorced, or widowed, could own land in their own name—even though they still did not have the right to vote and, in some states, did not have control over their own property.

To be sure, the land was free, but the fees and additional expenses were not. In the late 19th and early 20th century, filing fees ranged from $15.50 to $25, and the surveyor's fee to locate the claim and mark its boundaries cost from $30 to $100, depending on the size and location of the claim. On some claims, homesteaders had to buy water rights; this expense, along with maps and a notary fee, could come to $22. Other expenses could well bring the total cost up to several hundred dollars—a princely sum for women who, if they worked, earned an average of five to six dollars a week. As Florence Blake Smith, a homesteader in northeastern Wyoming, noted, "There would be filing fees, locating fees, transportation, price of lumber to build the required habitable house. Also, it seemed, one had to buy posts for fencing and the wire to string between them, all of which added to a prohibitive sum by the mile. Then on necessity, you had to eat to live, of course, during the slow process of homesteading."

But Smith was elated by the prospect of owning land: "the wonder of possession, the joy of looking out over one's land." Her shack measured 9 by 12 feet—"just the size of our living room rug at home"—and she furnished it with a walnut kitchen table, a cot, two kitchen chairs, a small rocker, and a regulation sheep-wagon stove. When necessary, she converted her bread can and the wooden boxes in which she shipped her canned goods into extra stools, and decorated her new home with delicate dotted Swiss curtains and a few pictures that she had brought from Chicago. The high cost of homesteading did not discourage women from doing so.

In early farm settlements, unmarried women and women who were heads of households represented about 5 percent of all homesteaders; after 1900, that number rose to about 20 percent. Women were as likely as men to succeed in making final claim to the land. Women homesteaders came from a variety of backgrounds. They included native-born Americans, Norwegians, Swedes, Danes, Finns, Dutch, Icelanders, Germans, Hungarians, Russians, Bohemians, Poles, Ukrainians, and Hispanic and African-American women. Women from a variety

Two women sit inside their shack in the Dakota Territory. Both married and unmarried women from a variety of cultural and economic backgrounds staked out claims in the West.

of religious backgrounds, such as Judaism, Catholicism, and the Presbyterian and Mormon faiths, staked homestead claims, either on their own or as part of a family unit.

Women's experiences as homesteaders were as diverse as their backgrounds. Although some women homesteaders became impoverished and dispirited, others had the good fortune, tenacity, or sheer stubbornness to turn their homesteading venture into a booming success. Laura Crews, who had grown up on a homestead in Kansas, entered the race for land on the Cherokee Strip in Oklahoma, which sold at $1.50 to $2.50 an acre. At the pop of a gun signaling the start of the race, Crews, along with 100,000 other land seekers, scrambled to stake a claim. On horseback, she rode 17 miles in 59 minutes and located a piece of land near a creek. There she set up her claim; she lived in a shelter she constructed, shoveled out a well, and subsisted at times on cornbread and rabbit stew. For years, her only income came from selling eggs at two cents a dozen—until oil was discovered on her land and she became a very wealthy woman.

Women homesteaded for many different reasons. Some women filed claims simply to increase their families' holdings;

Lena Carlson and her brother homesteaded next to each other in Benson County, North Dakota, in 1898. They shared a team of horses and farm equipment. Parents and adult children also took out adjoining claims. Whenever possible, families and friends who homesteaded came west together, tried to select neighboring quarter sections, and built their homes close to each other.

But many women homesteaders came alone, intending to settle in the West and work the land themselves or sell their

Building a home was the first order of business for all newcomers to the West. Where they settled determined the materials available for building.

claims later on to finance an education or start a dowry or nest egg. Anna and Emma Thingvold, two sisters who homesteaded in North Dakota in 1900, stayed on their claims only long enough to prove up, and then rented out their land. They used the income from the rent to open up a millinery and dressmaking shop in a town about 10 miles away from their claims.

Mary O'Kieffe, an overworked mother of nine, homesteaded to rid herself of a feckless husband who frequently disappeared, leaving his family to fend for themselves. One day in 1884, O'Kieffe had had enough and decided to take her children and find a homestead in western Nebraska. She directed her older children to make a cover for their farm wagon, which would serve as the family's traveling home, hitched up the work horses, and tied the milk cows on each side of the wagon. On the back, she hitched up the cultivator and a portable chicken coop that she had built to hold her rooster and two dozen hens. She and her children and their menagerie of farm animals embarked on the 500-mile journey, and after several mishaps and a few adventures they reached their new claim 51 days later. They built a sod house out of tightly packed chunks of dirt and mud, dug a well, and commenced a new life together.

Women also homesteaded for the adventure and for the opportunity to be independent. Abbie Bright of Kansas said that her "desire to cross the Mississippi and a love of traveling" prompted her to homestead. Lucy Goldthorpe, who left Iowa to homestead in North Dakota in 1905, believed that homesteading offered "one of the last opportunities to become a part of the development and growth of this great country." Gladys Belvie Whitaker, who homesteaded a 280-acre claim in Kern, California, took pride in being a property owner. "As I climbed down [from nailing shingles on her cabin roof], the sense of possession came strongly—that sense of ownership which is so much a part of us. It was all mine—I owned a house and land." Elinore Pruitt Stewart, who homesteaded a claim in Wyoming in the 1910s, wrote: "[A]ny woman who can stand her own company, can see the beauty of the sunset, loves growing things, and is willing to put in as much time at careful labor as she does over the washtub, will certainly succeed; will have independence, plenty to eat all the time, and a home of her own in the end." Stewart married one week after filing for her claim, which was adjacent to that of her husband's. Together, they managed a flourishing farm in which Elinore Pruitt Stewart cultivated a large vegetable garden. Her success in "growing things" and her pleasure in the beauty and bounty of the land bore out her claims of the many satisfactions found in homesteading.

Better economic opportunities, freedom and independence, a chance to visit new places—these were the main reasons why settlers went west. Others made the dangerous journey, oddly enough, to improve their health. The mild climate and clear, dry air of the Southwest and Pacific Northwest helped to cure tuberculosis and other diseases. In a last desperate attempt to rid herself of tuberculosis, Minnie Elliott moved to Scottsdale, Arizona, in the late 19th century with her two young children. Her doctor back East had given her six months to live. "At first," her daughter recalled, "Mother coughed so hard she could scarcely walk, but she gradually increased her breathing and bed exercises, finally dragging herself out into the desert to indulge instinctively in the daily, healing sunbath." Over time, Elliott walked longer distances, and after about a mile she would rest and "watch the glorious sunrises and drink in the rich, dry, healing desert breezes." Her daughter described Elliott's rapture in the desert landscape: "Soon the charm of those endless vistas broken here and there by fantastic buttes and mountains, tinted crimson and gold at daybreak, filled her soul with peace, and she learned to love her 'Desert of Hope.'" Minnie Elliott eventually gained 50 pounds, stopped coughing, organized a Sunday school, and became a well-respected reformer and health advocate in her tiny desert community.

The most popular route west was the Overland Trail—the dusty, mountainous pathway across the nation's interior, through what are now the states of Missouri, Nebraska, Wyoming, Idaho, Utah, Nevada, California, and Oregon. In the mid-1800s, the trail became a veritable highway to the gold mines of California, drawing eager gold seekers from across the

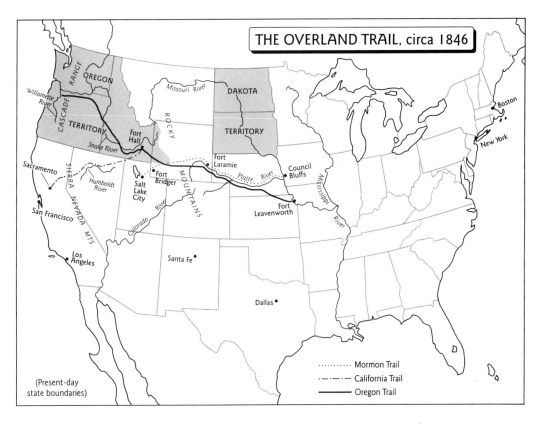

THE OVERLAND TRAIL, circa 1846

Boston
New York
OREGON
CASCADE RANGE
Willamette River
Missouri River
DAKOTA
TERRITORY
ROCKY MOUNTAINS
Fort Hall
Snake River
TERRITORY
Fort Laramie
Sacramento
Humboldt River
Salt Lake City
Fort Bridger
Platte River
Council Bluffs
San Francisco
SIERRA NEVADA MTS.
Colorado River
Fort Leavenworth
Mississippi River
Los Angeles
Santa Fe
Dallas

(Present-day state boundaries)

········· Mormon Trail
·—·—· California Trail
——— Oregon Trail

globe. From 1841 to 1866, almost two-thirds of the 350,000 people who moved west traveled by way of the Overland Trail.

In addition to the Overland Trail, there were a variety of ways to travel west. More affluent travelers could choose one of two seafaring routes: from ports of call along the eastern seaboard, down the Atlantic Ocean and across the Gulf of Mexico to Central America, then across by land to another port of embarkation and once again by ship to destinations in the far West. Other travelers went by sea all the way down the Atlantic Ocean to the southern tip of South America, across Cape Horn, and up the Pacific Ocean to the far West. The trip around this latter route cost approximately $600 per person, an amount beyond the means of many people who earned less than that in an entire year.

Most travelers from the East and Midwest chose the less expensive overland route. Who were these people? People of the middle class, neither very rich nor poor, and mostly white. Most emigrants had already made one or more moves in search of better land, or they were the children of parents who had moved before. They were used to uprooting themselves for a new start. Some settlers had owned or cleared land before, and most were young—between the ages of 16 and 35. The first gold rushers to converge on California were mostly men, but soon more families migrated to the gold fields and farmlands of California. In 1849, women comprised only 2 percent of California-bound migrants. By 1857, women made up half of the migrants of some wagon trains. Indeed, during the heaviest years of travel on the Overland Trail, from 1841 to 1866, most of the emigrants were families—and almost half of all emigrating families traveled with relatives. The 1850 Oregon census revealed that at least 40 percent of all households listed had kinship ties to at least one other household. Parents, siblings, aunts, uncles, and cousins followed each other west or hooked up together along the way. Many settlers, then, were fortunate enough to make the treacherous journey west within the comforting bosom of an extended family.

Black settlers journeyed as best they could—because most wagon trains forbade black passengers. The articles of incorporation of an 1843 Oregon company declared, "No Black or Mulatto person shall, in any case or any circumstances whatever, be admitted into this Society, or permitted to emigrate with it." Other westward-bound groups imposed the same restriction because of widespread prejudice against blacks. Some states and territories excluded blacks altogether. After Texas won its independence from Mexico in 1836, the republic's legislators passed several laws to re-enslave or expel free blacks there. In 1851, Indiana closed its borders to blacks, as did Illinois in 1853.

But blacks came however they could. Margaret Frink, a California-bound settler, wrote in her journal that somewhere in the desert she saw a "Negro woman...tramping along through the heat and dust, carrying a cast iron bake stove on her head, with her provisions and a blanket piled on top...bravely pushing on for California." Blacks who made it to the West also helped others to follow. Clara Brown, a former slave, became a washerwoman in Colorado. After the Civil War, she brought 34 relatives and sponsored other wagon trains out West.

Some blacks had lived out West from early on. Even before 1848, when the discovery of gold in California brought millions of gold seekers, the western region of the country had a sizable black population. In 1830, there were 13,000 freed slaves in the territories west of the Mississippi; by 1870, that number had risen to close to 45,000. Many went to California to look for gold. By 1849, black residents of San Francisco had formed a benefit and relief society of their own. By 1854, the city had three black churches, and over the next ten years three black-owned newspapers as well as more churches sprang up.

From 1878 to 1880, thousands of other black Americans headed for Kansas. Most of them were from the South, and they hoped to find in Kansas greater economic opportunity and freedom from prejudice. Some even immigrated in organized groups. By 1880, 15,000 black migrants in Kansas were trying to scratch out a living as farmers and laborers. Called Exodusters, they built huts made out of sod, or dirt, bricks and

From 1878 to 1880, thousands of Southern blacks, known as Exodusters, headed to Kansas in search of greater economic opportunity and a life free from the discrimination they faced in the South.

planted wheat. Some organized self-sufficient colonies or worked for white settlers as farm laborers or servants.

For most Exodusters, Kansas proved to be no refuge because of the isolation and unyielding land, and some moved on to Nebraska and Oklahoma or returned to the South. Luckier migrants managed to stay and make homes for themselves. Willianna Hickman, an Exoduster who migrated to Kansas from Kentucky in 1878, recalled that she cried from despair when she saw her new community, a collection of dugouts built against sloping dirt. But the "days, weeks, months, and years passed and I became reconciled to my home. We improved the farm and lived there for nearly twenty years." Outside of California and Kansas, black populations in the West remained small. In 1870, only 436 blacks lived in Colorado, 759 in Minnesota, 789 in Nebraska, and 172 in New Mexico.

Another beleaguered people who faced prejudice out West and created their own tight-knit communities were the Mormons. The Mormon religion was organized in 1830 by Joseph Smith, who claimed that he communicated with angels and received divine revelations. He published these revelations in the Book of Mormon. While gaining more followers, Mormons came under increasing attack by those who did not share their beliefs; to escape from this increasing prejudice, they moved from Ohio to Missouri and Illinois, and in 1847 to the valley of Salt Lake, Utah. There, under the leadership of Brigham Young, Smith's successor, they built a thriving community, with their own stores and home-based industries. By 1852, more than 20,000 Mormons had settled in and around Salt Lake City.

Though many Mormon precepts were basically conservative and uncontroversial, the Mormons' separateness, elaborate church hierarchy, and especially their practice of polygamy, in which one man married several women, evoked the wrath of non-Mormons. These critics believed that Mormon theology defied the separation of church and state, and that Mormon economic practices undermined free enterprise. But above all, they condemned the practice of polygamy. To them, polygamy challenged the ideals of family and true womanhood. Editorials, newspaper articles, novels, and plays depicted Mormon men as drunk, abusive husbands who beat and tortured their wives, and critics even compared polygamy to slavery.

Both settlers and critics back home regarded the Mormon church as a "sinister secret society" and Salt Lake a "sinful fallen city." Critics also viewed Mormon women either as degraded and brutalized by their husbands or as insane or immoral for accepting this "abominable system," which was the "ruin of domestic peace" and the "destroyer of all household affection." Mormon women were viewed as "harlots," "dull-witted hussies," "prostitutes and concubines."

Many settlers crossing into the far West carried with them such attitudes toward the Mormons. As much as they feared Indians, they also feared Mormons. Lavinia Porter, who had heard that "the Mormons never allowed a young woman to leave their borders," felt "decidely uneasy" until she was beyond Mormon settlements. Other travelers feared being attacked, especially after a combined Mormon and Indian force killed a non-Mormon emigrant company in 1857.

Even settlers who did not fear for their lives expressed their revulsion. Lucene Parsons, who spent the winter of 1851 in Salt Lake City before heading on to California, decided that "a meaner set lives not on this earth" and was convinced that any "honest person" would agree with her. After stopping in Salt Lake City in 1853, Harriet Sherrill Ward wrote in her journal, "They are a miserable lot of extortioners upon whom the wrath of God will yet be poured out." As she left Salt Lake City, she added, "The country through which we have passed today is beautiful and should be inhabited by a different set of beings than the Mormons."

Some settlers, however, were astute enough not to let their prejudices interfere with their admiration for the Mormons' industriousness and neat, thriving community life, in which women played a key social and economic role. Because Mormon families lived close together in tightly knit communities, they did not feel isolated and lonely as did homesteaders who lived on scattered farms. These closely arranged communities also

*Many people con-
demned the
Mormons' practice
of polygamy—
allowing a man to
have more than one
wife. Here, Alvin F.
Heaton (center)
stands with his two
wives and his chil-
dren and grand-
children.*

helped to hasten the spread of electricity. Between 1912 and
1922, the number of homes in Utah with electricity more than
doubled, and by 1930 only California and Massachusetts had
more farms with electricity than did Utah.

Although Mormon residents throughout Utah shared the
same religion, they did not share the same cultural backgrounds.
Mormon communities were astonishingly diverse, because the
Mormons pursued missionary work and encouraged a "gathering" of converts to the "Promised Land." In the last half of the
19th century, about 70 percent of the residents of Mormon
communities in the Salt Lake Valley of Utah were not born in
the United States. Instead, they had migrated from Scandinavia,
the British Isles, Switzerland, Germany, Italy, and France. One
village consisted mainly of Hawaiians, and a few hundred
Indians from the region had converted to the Mormon faith or
lived on farms established by Mormons.

For most women who ventured west, it was almost impossible to prepare for the journey. Guidebooks that began to

appear in the mid-1840s were far more informative about the tasks of which men took charge—how to purchase and equip a wagon, what clothes and tools to take, and where and how to break ground for camp and for grazing livestock. Beyond a list of foodstuffs, the guidebooks were mostly silent about women's trail chores—how to build a fire when no wood was available, or make a bed in a wagon or tent, or wash dishes and little ones without any water. On the trail, women learned these skills from other women or figured them out on their own.

The task of preparing and provisioning for the trip was laborious and time-consuming—indeed, sometimes longer than the journey itself. John and Cornelia Sharp and their seven children spent four years saving enough money to finance their overland journey. Even after all that, John had to borrow $500 from in-laws. Emigrants sold property holdings, farms, and household goods to finance their trips. In the weeks before they departed, their lives were a flurry of activity as they provisioned their traveling homes—their covered wagons. Women sewed dresses, trousers, sunbonnets, and other garments, as well as tents and wagon covers, and men purchased the supplies for the trip: livestock, wagons (unless they built them themselves), and tools.

The wagons needed to be small and light but durable enough to carry about 2,500 pounds and withstand rocky roads, steep mountain passes, and ferrying across streams and rivers. A typical wagon was about 10 feet long with 2-foot-high sideboards, and required 8 to 12 oxen yoked together in pairs. Wagons were covered in a double thickness of canvas and came with spare parts such as spokes, axles, and wheels in case one broke. Grease buckets, water barrels, and heavy rope were also essential equipment. The wagon and oxen, the most expensive items for the journey, cost about $400.

The 1845 edition of the *Emigrants Guide to Oregon and California* recommended that each wagon carry 200 pounds of flour, 150 pounds of bacon, 10 pounds of coffee, 20 pounds of sugar, and 10 pounds of salt. Along with other supplies, including rifles, gunpowder, and lead, the total cost of outfitting a

A wagon train carefully winds its way through a rocky patch on the journey out West. The wagons that settlers used had to be able to withstand many months of travel along these bumpy, rocky roads.

wagon came to almost $1,000, more than twice the average annual family income in the 1850s.

Some husbands and wives decided together to go west, but more often the husband made the decision and his wife had no choice but to go along. Margaret Hereford Wilson mournfully wrote to her mother in 1850, "Dr. Wilson has determined to go to California. I am going with him, as there is no other alternative.... Oh, my dear Mother...I thought that I felt bad when I wrote you...from Independence, but it was nothing like this."

Other women would not let their husbands go without them. When her husband wanted to set out for California's gold fields alone, Mary Jane Hayden crisply informed him, "We were married to live together. I am willing to go with you to any part of God's Foot Stool where you think you can do best, and under these circumstances you have no right to go where I cannot, and if you do you need never return for I shall look upon you as dead." The man dutifully delayed his journey until the next season, when his family could join him.

Settlers usually started their journey in mid- to late-April, after the muddy roads had begun to dry from winter snowfalls. If they lived east of the Missouri River, they first traveled to towns along the Missouri, such as Council Bluffs, Iowa. These settlements became known as "jumping off" places where settlers could replenish the supplies they had already used up, fix broken wagon parts or replace lame oxen, and organize themselves into wagon trains for the real journey ahead.

Today, travelers can cross the 2,400-mile stretch from the Missouri River to California in four days by car. By wagon, the journey often took seven months at a pace of 10 to 20 miles a day. Settlers who started out in mid-April did not reach their new homes in Oregon or California until November. They followed the Missouri River until it joined with the Platte River in what is now Nebraska. Then they followed along the Platte River through Nebraska and most of Wyoming Territories.

As more and more settlers journeyed west, guidebooks such as this appeared to advise travelers on what supplies they should take with them, what routes to avoid, and other helpful hints.

They passed landmarks such as Court House Rock, Chimney Rock, and Scotts Bluff. Settlers continued on through Sioux territory toward the 8,000-foot summit of the Rocky Mountains, up and over the easy grades of the mountain range to the South Pass, and on to Fort Bridger and Fort Hall in what is now Idaho. They had already endured torrid heat as well as golf ball–sized hail in the mountains—and they were only halfway there!

The road along the northern bank was variously called the Mormon Trail or the Nebraska City Road or California Road. After leaving Fort Hall, wagon trains often separated: Those headed for Oregon traveled north, following the Snake River to Fort Boise in Idaho Territory. Then they turned west, whereupon they scaled the sheer cliffs of the Blue Mountains. The wagons were hoisted up the cliffs by rope,

Maneuvering wagons over narrow, winding mountain trails took great skill and daring.

chains, winches, and pulleys, often with women and children trudging behind to put rocks behind the wagon wheels so they would not tumble down the mountainside. Wrote Helen Marnie Stewart: "The hills ware dreadful steep locking both wheels and coming down slow got down safe oh dear me. . . ." Settlers brought their wagons down over the mountains the same way.

After another 200 miles, the settlers reached the Columbia River, and most of them ferried the last 100 miles down the roiling waters into the fertile Willamette Valley. Some emigrants tied their possessions onto pack mules for the final leg of their journey, and others just abandoned everything they could not carry on their backs and, exhausted, walked the final miles of their journey.

California-bound settlers, eager to get to the Sacramento Valley before all the gold was gone, headed south from Fort Hall until they came to the Humboldt River in northeastern Nevada. They crossed 200 miles of scrappy, desertlike land, where the only vegetation they saw was dry grass, sagebrush, and prickly pear, and the only animals to be found were jackrabbits, coyotes, and rattlesnakes. Then they faced 50 more miles of travel through the harsh desert itself, under a broiling sun, with the sand whipping in their faces, before reaching the most grueling part of the journey—the slow, treacherous climb up the eastern slopes of the Sierra Nevada Mountains. Like Oregon-bound travelers, they had to maneuver their heavy wagonloads up the steep mountain passes with ropes, chains, and all the muscle they could muster.

The more foolhardy travelers, upon reaching Idaho or Nevada Territory, were tempted to try shortcuts. Men argued over what route to take, and even a scrap of paper nailed to a tree claiming to show a new road was enough to tempt travelers who were impatient or just plain exhausted to shorten their travel time. Some of these "shortcuts" proved to be longer and more arduous than the original route.

Despite the grueling nature of the journey, the Overland Trail was sometimes so populated that parts of it looked like a rush-hour highway of wagon trains. Amelia Stewart Knight, who was part of a wagon train in 1853, remarked at seeing more than 300 wagons waiting to cross the Elkhorn River in Nebraska Territory. "As far as the eye can reach," she wrote in her diary, "the bottom is covered, on each side of the river, with cattle and horses." After all the wagons in her train had crossed, she learned there were some 700 teams on the road ahead of them. "Hard times but they say misery loves company. We are not alone on these bare plains, it is covered with cattle and wagons."

Indeed, sometimes travelers fought to get ahead of each other. Knight reported that a driver from another wagon train actually brandished a pistol when one of the drivers from her train attempted to pass on the same road. Her train took a bypass to avoid any conflict, but later on when they stopped to rest and eat they saw the other team coming. "All [our] hands jumped for their teams saying they had earned the road too dearly to let them pass us again, and in a few moments we were all on the go again."

Others who came west did not cross the continental United States but endured an often harrowing journey from Asia or Europe by ship, traveling as long as two to six weeks at sea. From China and Japan, England, Ireland, France, Germany, Russia, Poland, Finland, Sweden, Norway, and Greece, immigrants came to seek better economic opportunities or flee repression.

Wong Ah So, who was born in China, came to the United States because she was a dutiful daughter. When her family could no longer make a living, her mother betrothed her, the eldest daughter, to Huey Yow, a Chinese laundry worker in California. "I was told by my mother that I was to come to the United States to earn money with which to support my parents and my family in Hong Kong." In 1922, she immigrated to San Francisco, prepared to be Huey Yow's wife and to earn money to help her family. "I thought that I was his wife, and was very grateful that he was taking me to such a grand, free country, where everyone was rich and happy," she later recalled.

Rachel Bella Calof, an immigrant Jew from Russia, journeyed by ship to New York City in 1894, and then traveled by train and wagon to a homestead in North Dakota. Calof planned to marry—sight unseen—another immigrant Jew who had already settled in America and who hoped to find prosperity by homesteading in North Dakota. As she embarked upon the first leg of her journey, a train trip to the port where she would sail to New York City, she was filled with fear and sorrow at leaving her family behind, "knowing that in all probability I would never see them again.… I knew nothing about my final destination. The nature of the lands or the great ocean I would cross were unknown to me. Above all, my welfare was in the hands of a man half a world away, whom I knew only by name and a photographic picture."

Calof and her future husband were part of a major eastern European Jewish exodus to the West. As early as 1849, immigrant Jews from Europe started flocking to the gold fields of California, along with Japanese, German, Italian, and other immigrants who hoped to get rich quickly. They soon fanned out beyond California to Oregon, Nevada, Montana, Colorado, Utah, and New Mexico. Later on, between 1880 and 1930, Jewish homesteaders, usually sponsored and financed by Jewish religious and charitable agencies, settled mostly in North and South Dakota, Wisconsin, Michigan, Illinois, and Kansas and Nebraska. From their sponsors they received enough money to carry them through the first hard winter and spring planting season.

For east European Jews, like Mormons, a farm in America represented social, economic, and religious freedom. Throughout Russia, Jews could not own land, and so were forced to live in crowded towns, where they often worked in regimented factories. Nor could they practice their religion freely because of the bitter hatred of their non-Jewish neighbors: In Russia, Jewish homes and businesses were routinely destroyed in government-sponsored attacks. A farm in the New World symbolized economic opportunity, a chance to breath clean air and take control of one's destiny, and a haven from violence and hatred. But for Calof and thousands of other immigrant homesteaders, the reality was years of hard work and poverty before they were able to comfortably sustain themselves on the land.

Because most immigrants had very little money, or wanted to save whatever money they had for starting their new life in America, they traveled the cheapest way possible—in steerage, a section below deck with the worst accommodations. They stayed together in overcrowded, airless rooms with bunks stacked one on top of the other like logs. The food usually consisted of moldy, soggy bread and thin, watery soup. Jewish immigrants who observed kosher dietary laws could not even eat this.

Although men and women had separate toilet facilities, they sometimes shared one washroom, with basins that served as bathtubs, laundry tubs, and dishpans. Israel Kasovich, who immigrated from eastern Europe in the early 1900s, described the nightmare of the journey: "We were all herded together in a dark, filthy compartment in the steerage.... Seasickness broke out among us. Hundreds of people had vomiting fits, throwing up even their mother's milk.... The confusion of cries became unbearable.... I wanted to escape from that inferno but no sooner had I thrust my head forward from the lower bunk than someone above me vomited straight upon my head."

Most ships docked in New York harbor, and immigrants continued their journey by train or stagecoach. But some ships docked at other ports around the United States, such as Boston, Philadelphia, Chicago, and Galveston, Texas. San Francisco's Angel Island was the port of entry for most Chinese, Japanese, and Koreans. From these points, immigrants made their way to their final destinations—after being subjected to a barrage of questioning and examination by U.S. immigration officials. These officials wanted to confirm that they were not carrying any communicable or disabling diseases, were neither criminals nor revolutionaries out to overthrow the U.S. government, and were able to work or had friends or relatives who could support them.

Rachel Bella Calof, who disembarked at Ellis Island in New York City, found the scrutiny of immigration officials to be the most frightening part of her journey over. She recalled that she

The discovery of gold in California in 1848 attracted many young Chinese men who hoped to strike it rich. Chinese women soon followed.

and her fellow immigrants were ushered "into an enormous room with bars across the windows which aroused considerable apprehension because it seemed so like a jail. With a word or gesture from an official, one standing a few feet from the gate opening to the golden land could be refused entry after having traveled so far."

Chinese women faced especially strong resistance. Though other immigrants could enter the United States right away if they met American immigration standards, Chinese women were detained for up to several weeks while officials determined their eligibility to enter the country under special laws restricting Chinese immigration. The laws required that Chinese women show evidence that they were not prostitutes. These laws reflected a deep-seated prejudice against the Chinese.

At Angel Island in 1903, Mai Zhouyi, a missionary from Canton and the wife of a Chinese merchant in San Francisco, was locked in a shed for 40 days while immigration officials verified her status. "All day long I faced the walls and did nothing except eat and sleep like a caged animal."

Unlike European immigrants, who fanned out across the West, Chinese and Japanese immigrants, with some exceptions, mostly migrated to California. During the late 19th century and well into the 20th, most Japanese settled in San Francisco.

Others went to the California towns of Sacramento and Fresno. Some headed for other western towns such as Portland, Oregon; Seattle, Washington; and Salt Lake City. The California gold rush attracted young, unmarried Chinese men hoping to seek their fortune—and their arrival, in turn, created a demand for young Chinese women.

In China, young, unsuspecting women were tricked or lured by "agents" who promised them a better way of life in America. Upon arrival in San Francisco, they were turned over to men who had already paid for them, or sold to the highest bidder. Most of them were forced to work as prostitutes, and they lived as virtual prisoners. In 1860, about 85 percent of the Chinese women in San Francisco were prostitutes; by 1880, the number had declined to 21 percent because of stricter immigration policies and because former prostitutes had married and had renounced prostitution. In this early period, a few Chinese wives came to join their husbands in fishing communities near San Francisco.

By the mid-19th century, the West was the most ethnically diverse region of the United States, a mosaic of inhabitants from across the globe. From 1860 to 1900, between one-third and one-fourth of the western population had been born in another country. In 1890, North Dakota's population was about 44 percent foreign-born. Immigrants to North Dakota included large numbers of Norwegians, Russians, Canadians, Germans, and Swedes. Only one out of every five North Dakotans was a native-born American child of native-born American parents.

But this mosaic of peoples from different cultures and ethnic backgrounds was far from harmonious. White Christian settlers viewed those of a different skin color or religion—Native American, black, Hispanic, Chinese, Japanese, Jewish, Irish, Mormon—with a mixture of arrogance and contempt. Friendships occasionally blossomed between people from different cultural backgrounds. Far more common, however, was the hostility and exclusion that immigrant settlers faced from white settlers, who brought with them the social, political, and economic power of the U.S. government.

The history of Chinese and Japanese immigration, in particular, is a sorry tale of cruelty, prejudice, and intolerance. Chinese miners and other laborers were the targets of resentful white workers who believed they were taking all of the gold and work available. Special taxes were imposed on Chinese workers. The California legislature passed laws that denied Chinese residents basic rights, including the right to testify in court, seek employment in public works jobs, intermarry with whites, and own land. Chinese were barred from better-paying jobs in mines, factories, fisheries, and agriculture, and could not live outside of Chinatown in San Francisco or send their children to public schools.

In the 1870s and 1880s, prejudice against the Chinese rose to a crescendo. Throughout the West, Chinese settlements were attacked, looted, and burned by rampaging mobs. In Los Angeles in 1871, unarmed Chinese were shot during a riot, and others were yanked out of their homes and beaten or murdered. In 1885, a mob of white miners massacred 28 Chinese at the mining settlement of Rock Springs, Wyoming.

In 1882, the Chinese Exclusion Act severely restricted the number of Chinese women who could enter the United States

Chinese women detained at the immigration station at Angel Island in San Francisco Bay ponder their future. Harsh immigration restrictions limited the number of Chinese allowed to enter the United States.

and blocked the immigration of all Chinese laborers for a period of 10 years. It defined laborers as "both skilled and unskilled laborers and Chinese employed in mining," and exempted merchants, diplomats, and other nonlaborers. Subsequent laws continued to restrict the entry of both Chinese and Japanese immigrants.

Korean immigrants also encountered vicious prejudice. Unlike Chinese or Japanese immigrants, many Koreans went first to Hawaii, where they labored on sugar plantations and eventually opened their own businesses, or resettled in San Francisco. Some also ventured into other western states.

Like other immigrants who fled government oppression, many Koreans came to escape the tyranny of Japanese rulers who had taken over their country. But they often found hostility in their new homeland as well. Mary Paik was five years old when her family arrived in California. They had barely stepped on shore when they were confronted by a group of young white men who "laughed at us and spit in our faces," she reported.

Mary Paik's family moved to southern California to live and work in a citrus grove. Like other people of color—Japanese, Chinese, Hispanic, and African American—they were prohibited from residing in town with white people and were instead forced to live in a one-room shack with no gas, electricity, or running water. This shack was part of a migrant camp on the outskirts of town.

On her first day of school, Mary Paik was taunted by her white classmates, who formed a circle around her and sang:

"Ching chong, Chinaman,
Sitting on a wall.
Along came a white man,
And chopped his head off."

As they sang, each child in turn struck Mary on the back of her neck.

"For Whites Only" signs hung everywhere, said Paik—on public restrooms, on theaters, swimming pools, barbershops, and other businesses. Even the minister of a local church barred her from attending. When she and her brothers, who were

Presbyterian, attempted to enter the church, the minister put his arm across the door. "I don't want dirty Japs in my church," he sneered at her. The young girl calmly responded, "Would it make any difference if I told you we are not Japanese, but Korean?" He said, "What the hell's the difference? You all look alike to me."

Whether settlers came from halfway around the world or from the American heartland, they were beckoned westward by dreams of a better life for themselves and their families. The last hurdle before departing on their journey was saying good-bye to friends and relatives. Leave-taking was a wrenching beginning to the journey west. Little Mary Paik begged her grandmother to leave Korea and come with her family, but the old woman refused. Abby E. Fulkerath, who emigrated west from Ohio in 1863 after the deaths of several children, found it hard to say good-bye to her relatives, but harder still "to leave my children buried in graveyards."

The journey west was intended to be a new beginning, to a land of opportunity and a life of prosperity. But emigrants' high hopes were mixed with a deep sense of loss. In an age of precarious long-distance communication, before telephones, jet travel, and reliable mail delivery, emigrants said good-bye as if they were crossing a great divide from the familiar past into an uncertain future. As their ships set sail or their wagons hit the dusty roads, they no doubt wondered if they would ever see family and friends again. Lodisa Frizzell, pondering these sad thoughts, confided in her diary, en route to California in 1852, "[T]he wellknown voices of our friends still ring in our ears, the parting kiss feels still warm upon our lips, and that last separating word Farewell! sinks deeply into the heart. It may be the last we ever hear from some or all of them, and to those who start…there can be no more solemn scene of parting only at death."

On the journey
west, women often
drove the wagons
while the men
went ahead to
scout trails.

CHAPTER 3

"YOU WILL WONDER HOW I CAN BEAR IT"

LIFE ON THE OVERLAND TRAIL

S hortly after arriving at her claim in Burnt Fork, Wyoming, homesteader Elinore Pruitt Stewart took her young daughter, Jerrine, on an overnight campout in the wilderness. She found a suitable clearing to set up camp and unpacked their provisions for the night, then made a roaring campfire. Later she proudly wrote to a former employer, "I kept thinking how superior I was since I dared to take such an outing when so many poor women down in Denver were bent on making their twenty cents per hour in order that they could spare a quarter to go to the 'show.' I went to sleep with a powerfully self-satisfied feeling."

Stewart expressed a glowing pride and sense of freedom that many women felt in the expanses of the West. On the arduous overland journey and in the task of creating new homes and communities, some women broke free from the constraints that had shaped their lives back home and marshaled new skills and inner resources. But other women craved the traditional domestic pattern of their former lives and found the hardships of homesteading so overwhelming that they had neither the time nor energy to try out new ways of living.

In the early decades of the 19th century, American women's social and economic roles underwent a profound change. As the nation relied more on factories to produce household goods, such as clothing, candles, soap, and foods, middle-class women no longer spent most of their waking hours making such items for their families. Instead, they had more free time to devote to charitable activities. In the three decades before the Civil War, many middle- and upper-class women joined religious and social reform organizations. These organizations included local relief societies that assisted ill or destitute women as well as local and regional groups that worked for the abolition of slavery or a ban on the consumption of alcohol. Such community activism expanded women's awareness of the world beyond their front doors and inspired them to develop valuable leadership skills. But their newfound activism did not change their or other people's expectations of their basic social roles. From magazine articles to ministers' sermons, women were told that their fundamental goal in life was to be a loving wife and mother, and to create a pious, nurturing home. In general, women were prevented from getting a rigorous academic education, pursuing an occupation beyond that of homemaker or teacher, and deciding for themselves how they wanted to live.

For women in a wagon train chugging along dusty trails and winding precariously through treacherous mountain passes, creating a clean, healthy, and morally upright home was a seemingly insurmountable task. But, in trying to uphold high domestic standards on the trail, women often discovered new inner resources and ingenuity. Indeed, many women found comfort and reassurance in performing traditional domestic duties, even under such trying conditions, because these tasks reminded them of home and routine. They learned to cook over an open fire, often in the rain or wind, or while warding off flies and other insects. Oftentimes, their "oven" consisted of two forked sticks driven into the ground with a pole laid across. From the pole swung a heavy kettle or pot, which more often than not fell into the fire. Families gamely ate meals that were burnt or full of dirt.

Other women dug a trench about one foot deep and three feet long, and hung a crane over the trench with a coffee pot and camp kettle. Either form of cooking, as Lodisa Frizzell wryly commented, "goes agin the grain." Esther Hannah, an 18-year-old minister's wife who emigrated west in 1852, described the ordeal of cooking at night in bone-chilling wind: "It is very trying on the patience to cook and bake on a little green wood fire with the smoke blowing in your eyes so as to blind you, and shivering with cold so as to make the teeth chatter."

Cooking in the rain was especially difficult because the dried weeds and buffalo chips—dried cow dung—would not burn. James Clyman, a settler, described one woman in his wagon train who, during a downpour, "watched and nursed the fire and held an umbrella over the fire and her skillet with the greatest composure for near 2 hours and baked enough bread to give us a very plentiful supper." Even in mild weather cooking was a time-consuming process. Women and children had the unenviable task of gathering dry grasses and buffalo chips to

Gathering buffalo chips—dried cow dung—to use as fuel was a messy but necessary chore before cooking could begin.

use as fuel. Women who had prided themselves back home on their gentility found themselves out in the fields picking up dried manure. At first they wore gloves, but they soon discarded them as a nuisance.

Buffalo chips burned quickly and needed constant replenishing. Charley O'Kieffe, a boy at the time, described the many steps his mother followed just to bake biscuits: "Stoke the stove, get out the flour sack, stoke the stove, wash your hands, mix the biscuit dough, stoke the stove, wash your hands, cut out the biscuits with the top of a baking-powder can, stoke the stove, wash your hands, put the pan of biscuits in the oven, keep on stoking the stove until the biscuits are done. Mother had to go through this tedious routine three times a day excepting when what she was cooking did not require the use of the oven."

But perhaps the most challenging part of cooking was trying to introduce some variety into meals. The usual breakfast fare was bread or pancakes, fried meat, beans, and tea or coffee. Pancakes were made with flour, water, and baking soda, and were cooked in a large frying pan. The midday meal and dinner usually consisted of beans, bread, and bacon. Cecilia Adams, who migrated from Illinois to Oregon in 1852, wrote that one Sunday in June she had "cooked beans and meat, stewed apples and baked suckeyes [pancakes]…besides making Dutch cheese." Some women packed dried fruit to prevent scurvy, a debilitating disease caused by the lack of vitamin C, but many settlers did not and suffered from scurvy on the journey. Other women packed canned oysters, a few eggs, molasses, and tomato catsup to add mealtime variety, and most migrants supplemented their diets with freshly caught game and fish.

Still, settlers often endured dry patches where there were no creeks to fish in or no game to be found, and mealtime was utterly uninspiring. As Helen Carpenter, bound for California in 1857, remarked in her diary, "One does like a change and about the only change we have from bread and bacon is to bacon and bread."

Cooking was only one of many chores women performed on the trail. They also packed and repacked bedding and tents at each campsite, which usually meant every night; mended their family's clothing and patched up torn spots on the wagon canvas; collected berries; cleaned and aired wagons; cared for their children and the ill; and did the family washing. This last task, like cooking, was particularly onerous in the outdoors. Oftentimes, women had to lug clothes a long way to the nearest riverbank, and withstand a broiling sun or biting wind as they washed. Rebecca Ketcham, a settler from Ithaca, New York, bound for Oregon, recorded in her diary, "Camilla and I both burnt our arms very badly while washing. They were red and swollen and painful as though scalded with boiling water. Our hands are blacker than any farmer's and I do not see that there is any way of preventing it, for everything has to be done in the wind and sun." For Caroline Richardson, however, washing was more pleasant: "[w]ashed by full moon in river," she recorded in her diary. "Beau[tiful]."

Watching children on the trail was also harder than it was back home. Because the adult members of many families were young when they set out for the West, almost every married woman traveled with small children—and about one out of every five women was pregnant during the journey. At night and during layovers, small children had to be supervised constantly to keep them from falling into the campfire or wandering off. Margaret Frink, bound for California from Indiana in 1850, thought she had lost her son after the boy found a horse and galloped away from their camp. When it came time for the wagons to leave again, the boy was nowhere to be found. His mother panicked, for she was afraid Indians would capture him. She recalled later, "To increase my agony a company of packers [told of passing 500 Indians]. I suffered the agony almost of death in a few minutes." She begged the packers to turn around and help look for her son, but they had to push ahead. "The thought of leaving the boy, never to hear him again! But just at dark, Aaron [her husband] came in sight having the lost boy with him. My joy turned to tears!"

While the wagons rolled along, children became squirmy, and mothers had to keep them from climbing or falling over the

Camps along the Overland Trail offered travelers a brief respite from the rigors of their journey. On layover days, travelers caught up on chores such as cooking and cleaning and managed to enjoy a little relaxation.

side. Although older children often helped with trail chores, such as gathering buffalo chips and watching the livestock, they, too, had to be supervised. And children of all ages came down with the usual childhood illnesses—measles, chickenpox, whooping cough, and scarlet fever—as well as more deadly diseases such as cholera, smallpox, and typhoid fever.

The rugged conditions of the trail itself also played havoc with children's health. Bedding and clothes soaked during storms, extreme heat and chilly winds, and poor food lowered the body's resistance and made both children and adults susceptible to fevers and chills that could easily turn into pneumonia. Few wagon trains included doctors, so mothers became the doctors in their families. Women relied on commercial medicines such as laudanum and camphor or home remedies such as herbs and water baths. But these were feeble weapons against diseases that spread like wildfire among travelers weakened by fatigue, poor diets, sharing beds, and unsterile utensils. Margaret Irvin remembered how "worried my mother was when any of us got sick" because "there were no doctors in the party and all we had to doctor ourselves with were the few medicines we brought along and the home remedies we knew about, such as tying a strip of bacon around our necks when we had a sore throat or blowing sulphur down our throats."

Trail conditions were not only a challenge to keeping children safe and calm; they also threatened women's every notion of civilized womanhood. Although some women dressed in durable, dark-colored homespun or even wore bloomers—pantaloons under a calf-length skirt—others insisted on wearing what they had worn back home: ribbons and bows and starched white aprons and petticoats. Miriam Davis Colt, who settled in Kansas with her husband and children in 1856, wondered if she was becoming uncivilized because of her disheveled appearance. "I have cooked so much out in the sun and smoke that I hardly know who I am," she wrote in her diary, "and when I look into the little looking glass I ask, 'Can this be me?'"

For women, then, days—and most nights—on the trail were a round of cooking, cleaning, washing, and child care under the most trying of conditions. Charlotte Stearns Pengra, who migrated west from New England in 1853, recorded a litany of chores in her diary: "April 29, 1853: I hung out what things were wet in the waggon, made griddle cakes, stewed berries and made tea for supper. After that was over made two loaves of bread stewed a pan of apples prepared potatoes and meat for breakfast, and mended a pair of pants for Wm. pretty tired.... May 8: baked this morning and stewed apples this afternoon commenced washing...got my white clothes ready to suds.... I feel very tired and lonely."

Some tasks were harder to complete on the trail, but some were also easier. There were no floors to scrub, no food-encrusted iron stoves to clean out, and no ironing to do because women allowed themselves the luxury of skipping that task.

Even churning butter required less effort: Women churned their butter while the wagons rolled along, letting the physical motion of the wagon churn for them. During the day, as the wagons lumbered along the trail, women had more time to sit and write letters, catch up on mending or knitting, read or write in their diaries, visit with other women who joined them in their wagons, or just sit and stare out at the passing scenery. Nancy Hunt, an emigrant to California, recalled that she "alternatively drove [the wagon] and dozed, talked and meditated."

Women's work on the trail varied according to where they came from and what social and economic class they belonged to. Helen Carpenter, a newlywed who spent her honeymoon journeying to California, observed, "If they [women] are Missourians they have the milking to do if they are fortunate enough to have cows. I am lucky in having a Yankee for a husband, so am well waited on."

Other women simply balked at doing their fair share. Emma Tate recalled a woman in her wagon train who "refused to help the other women at cooking and camp work, in fact would not even comb her children's hair." Instead, she sat on the edge of the wagon and nagged her husband while he did all of the chores.

At the beginning of the journey, women performed all of the traditional domestic tasks while men drove the wagons, cared for the livestock, chose roads and campsites, ferried the wagons and livestock across rivers, hunted game for meals, and stood guard at night. As the trip wore on, and wagon trains split up or hired hands quit, women and men shared more responsibilities. Men helped with the cooking and washing, helped unpack and repack tents and bedding, and set up sleeping quarters. In turn, women helped to scout out the trail or find a suitable spot to camp for the night, pitched tents, yoked the oxen and drove the teams, unloaded wagons to ferry them across rivers and then reloaded them on the other side, and stood guard against attacks by Indians or wild animals. Women assumed all responsibilities when their husbands became ill or died or were simply away on hunting expeditions.

Beyond the day-to-day hardships, weather conditions along the Overland Trail provided many an obstacle to a traveler's peace of mind and ease of travel. On May 9, 1853, Amelia Stewart Knight recorded in her diary that they crossed the Elkhorn River in Nebraska Territory in freezing temperatures. Three days later, the weather was "beautiful," but the roads "very dusty." The next day, May 13, they crossed the river again at another point and had breakfast on the other side in ankle-deep sand with the wind blowing all around—"them that eat the most breakfast eat the most sand," Knight commented ruefully. On May 16, they had "all kinds of weather...[t]his morning was dry, dusty and sandy. This afternoon it rained, hailed, and the wind was very high. Have been traveling all the afternoon in mud and water up to our hubs. Broke chains and stuck in the mud several times." And so her diary continues. Torrid heat, freezing rain and hail, high winds, snow up in the mountains, and other hazardous weather conditions followed them across the trail to the end of their journey.

River crossings posed some of the worst obstacles. Every time a wagon train crossed the river—as well as after heavy rains when wagons got stuck in the mud—each wagon had to be unpacked for easier movement and then repacked on the other side. For river crossings, wagon wheels were removed and the wagon beds were put on flatboats, which were attached by a pulley to a rope stretched across the river to prevent them from being carried downstream. Even so, the flatboats often landed far afield down the opposite shore and had to be towed upstream to the landing before their loads could be removed. Settlers tied ropes to their oxen's horns and mules' necks to help them face the current as they swam across the river. The settlers ferried themselves across in rafts or canoes—often in churning, roiling waters with the wind whipping overhead. River crossings were among the most harrowing and complicated parts of the journey. Catherine Haun, a young bride from Iowa, recorded that it took her caravan of 70 wagons a week to get across the Missouri River.

River crossings were dangerous and time-consuming affairs for wagon trains. Each wagon had to be unpacked, partly dismantled, and ferried across the river on a flat-boat—often in treacherous weather conditions.

Early in the journey, women confronted the loneliness of life on the trail. For Helen Stewart, the chirping of the whip-poorwills sadly reminded her of "our old farm in pensillvania the home of my childhood where I have spent the happiest days I will ever see again.... I feel rather lonesome today oh solitude solitude how I love it if I had about a dozen of my companions to enjoy it with me."

It was not at all unusual for Stewart and other women to confide in their journals rather than to their husbands. Throughout the journey to California, Lavinia Porter wrote, she would "make a brave effort to be cheerful and patient until the camp work was done." But when she felt overwhelmed, she would go off by herself and "throw myself down on the unfriendly desert and give way like a child to sobs and tears, wishing myself back home with my friends and chiding myself for consenting to take this wild goose chase." Even so, these periodic outbursts did not ease the growing tension between her and her husband: "James and I had gradually grown silent and taciturn and had unwittingly partaken of the gloom and somberness of the dreary landscape." But however much women lamented the hardships, they accepted them. As Margaret Hereford Wilson wrote to her mother in 1850, "You will wonder how I can bear it, but it is unavoidable, and I have to submit without complaining."

Occasionally women did rebel. Porter refused to stay at a dirty campsite picked out by the men in her wagon train and forced her husband to move to a cleaner spot. "The other women," she recalled, "looking on my daring insubordination with wondering eyes, and envious of my cleanly quarters, at last plucked up courage to follow my example, and with much profanity the camp was moved." Cora Agatz's mother may have averted a bloody confrontation with a group of Indians by refusing to obey an order to move the wagons into a circle and prepare to fight. "Captain Hill," she told the leader of the train, "I know you are the master of this train, but I refuse to obey you for you know as well as I that we are in no condition to fight these Indians." The captain reluctantly agreed, and the Indians went on their way.

For pregnant women and new mothers, life on the trail was even harder. Twelve days before she gave birth, Amelia Stewart Knight was climbing up and down rocky hills, trudging through mud holes, bending over a washtub or campfire, and reacting to the stench of dead, rotting livestock left by the roadside. Many women, like Knight, were in the final stages of pregnancy during the journey and had no choice but to give birth on the trail. In the best of conditions, for women who could afford a doctor's care in a sanitary setting, childbirth in the 19th century could be dangerous because physicians were ill-informed and unequipped to treat complications. But on the Overland Trail it was a nightmare. Women gave birth in cramped, damp wagons, usually with no doctor available and little water at hand. Some wagon trains stopped for only a day, long enough for other women in the caravan to assist in the delivery, then pushed on. The mother and her newborn spent the most precarious recovery days in a jostling wagon, bumping over rocky paths or climbing up steep mountain passes.

Lucy Henderson Deadly recalled how her younger sister died when she unwittingly drank a whole bottle of laudanum, a potent painkiller, that hung from a sideboard in the family's wagon. Three days later, still grieving for one daughter, her mother gave birth to another little girl. The wagon train stopped long enough for the delivery, then went on. "The going was terribly rough," Lucy recalled. "The men walked beside the wagons and tried to ease the wheels down into the rough places, but in spite of this it was a very rough ride for my mother and her new born babe."

Amidst all of the hardships, the specter of Indian ambushes weighed heavily on settlers. Americans went west with many preconceptions about Indians, mostly ones filled with fear and condemnation. They first encountered Native Americans in the outfitting towns in Iowa and Kansas. The Indians in these towns, mostly Winnebagos, Pawnees, and Delaware, had already been displaced from their lands by previous waves of settlers or by government troops and were often homeless and reduced to begging. Settlers did not understand that when Indians offered them a token of hospitality, they were expected to respond in kind. Instead, they castigated the Indians who came up to their wagons as "beggars" and "thieves." Settlers also decried the Indians' inability to speak English. Sniffed Rebecca Ketcham, en route to Oregon, "They do not understand any of our language, and when they can speak a word of it they seem to think that they have done something very smart."

The settlers' bias against Indians is reflected in the white women's descriptions of them as "cruel," "savage," "immoral," "of a lower order," "untrustworthy," "thieving," "very cowardly," and "ignorant and simple." When Indians helped retrieve her wagon train's lost horses, Rebecca Ketcham reacted with surprise and condescension, writing, "That they were honest enough to be bringing the lost horses to us we could hardly believe."

To be sure, there were isolated Indian assaults and ambushes on the trail. Mary Perry Frost, who journeyed to Oregon Territory with her parents during the summer of 1854, witnessed an ambush in which both her father and uncle were killed. At first, a group of Indians approached their small wagon train in a friendly manner, "shaking hands and asking for whiskey," recalled Mary. "Upon being told that we had none they began to talk of trading with the men." Suddenly, without warning, "they opened fire on us, shooting my father, my uncle, and my father's teamster." The Indians also killed some of the other travelers, "leaving a boy fourteen with an arrow in his chest."

More common than these violent incidents were simple acts of misunderstanding. Indians often strode up to camps or homesteads uninvited. Some women, misunderstanding their intentions, brandished weapons such as brooms, revolvers, or knives, while others offered a trinket or piece of food to get them to leave. One Comanche Indian tried to trade his clothes to Ella Bird Dumont for a rifle he wanted. Neither of them understood the other's language. When he began to take off his clothes, Dumont blushed with embarrassment. Her husband came and cleared up the misunderstanding, and they all had a good laugh.

Far more settlers died from disease and accidents than from Indian attacks. Death was an inescapable part of life on the trail. From 1849 to 1854, outbreaks of cholera plagued the nation and followed settlers west. Some large wagon trains lost as many as two-thirds of their travelers. Settlers who helped bury the dead were themselves struck down within a matter of days. During an epidemic of cholera along the Platte River in June 1852, Jane Kellogg recorded in her diary, "All along the road up the Platte River was a grave yard; most any time of day you could see people burying their dead; some places five or six graves in a row.... It was a sad sight; no one can realize it unless they had seen it."

Some families escaped illness along the way, but disease and death hung over other families like an unwelcome intruder. The family of William Smith migrated first from Iowa to Missouri and then hitched up their "Prairie Schooner" in 1846 for Oregon. On the journey, Smith died of a heart attack, leaving a wife and nine children, one of whom was near death and another seriously injured from an earlier accident.

After burying her husband, Ellen Smith packed up her children and took her place as head of the family. The harsh weather and rough roads further weakened the sick child, Louisa. When she knew that she was dying, Louisa asked her mother to bury her in a "Grave six feet deep" so that the wolves would not eat her—a concern shared by many other overlanders after passing graves that had been raided by wild animals. When Louisa finally died, her mother chose a "prity little Hill" on which to bury her, and the men in her company began digging Louisa's grave. Because their tools were so crude, the digging was hard and they wanted to stop at four feet. But, heeding her daughter's last request, Ellen Smith insisted that the hole be two feet deeper and she got down in the grave and began to dig it herself. Her brother-in-law, unable to bear the sight of a mother digging her child's grave, assured her that the

Many of those who set out for the West never made it and were buried along the trail. This stone marks the grave of Amanda, the consort of M. J. Lamin, who died of cholera in 1850 somewhere in Colorado.

men would finish the job. The wagon train pushed on, and Ellen Smith trudged on foot, leading her eight surviving children, the smaller ones tied to an ox. With their provisions exhausted, the family subsisted on wood mice until an army pack train brought more provisions. Ellen Smith and her children reached Salem, Oregon, on December 23, 1846, and they cleared the land and built a house on their 640-acre claim.

Perhaps the most famous catastrophe on the trail was the ordeal of the ill-fated Donner Party. Starting out from Illinois in 1846, the wagon train, led by George Donner, divided into two groups. Donner led a group of about 20 wagons over an unknown cutoff around the south side of Great Salt Lake. Because of unexpected hindrances along the way, they reached the Sierra Nevada Mountains as winter set in. Snow blocked their way through the range, and they were forced to set up camp. Once again, the caravan split up, and one group built cabins on Truckee Lake in the eastern Sierras while the others set up camp five miles away. By December, their food supplies had run out and, facing starvation, 17 members tried to cross the Sierras on snowshoes—among them, 7 survived. They and the rest of the survivors staved off starvation by eating the bodies of their dead comrades. Altogether, 40 of the 87 emigrants managed to survive, and were rescued by four relief teams that plucked them out of the mountains.

Thirteen-year-old Virginia Reed, one of the survivors, wrote her cousin after the ordeal, "We had to kill little cash [their family dog]…and eat him; we at his head and feet & hide & evry thing about him. O Mary I would cry and wish I had what you all wasted."

Sickness and death, along with glorious vistas and intoxicating freedom, entwined the overland journey like the fragrant but thorn-encrusted wild roses that grew along the way. Celinda Hines, part of a wagon train from Oswego County, New York, in 1853, watched her father drown while crossing a river with their wagon; because they had not wanted to use their dwindling funds on ferry passage, the men tried to swim the cattle across. Her father got caught in a swift current and his body was never found. "With hearts overflowing with sorrow we were under the necessity of pursuing our journey immediately, as there was no grass where we were," Celinda wrote. She comforted herself with the thought that her father was "yet living" and would "watch over me and continue to guide me."

No wonder that travelers became preoccupied with the accidents and illness that plagued them throughout the journey. Women, especially, kept a careful count in their diaries of the mishaps—and also of the graves they passed along the way. En route to Oregon, Cecilia Adams of Illinois recorded the number of graves she saw with the precision of a bookkeeper:

June 25 Passed 7 graves...made 14 miles

June 26 Passed 8 graves

June 29 Passed 10 graves

June 30 Passed 10 graves...made 22 miles

July 1 Passed 8 graves...made 21 miles

July 2 One man of [our] company died. Passed 8 graves . . .

  made 16 miles

Lodisa Frizzell, who had likened saying good-bye to the finality of death, lived with a constant, gnawing fear of danger on the journey. She "dreamed of being attacked by wolves and bears," and by the time her wagon train reached the South Pass of the Rockies she was downright morbid. "The heart has a thousand misgivings," she confided to her diary, "and the mind is tortured with anxiety & often as I passed the fresh made graves, I have glanced at the side boards of the waggon, not knowing how soon it might serve as a coffin for some one of us."

The wrong turn, a broken axle, an injured draft animal, a lost child or a layover to recover from illness or pregnancy, fear of Indian attacks or actual assaults, even bad weather—these and so many other mishaps plagued travelers. Despite all of the hardship, however, men and women found moments of respite, even pleasure, on the trail. Crossing the Great Plains or the desert could be monotonous after endless days of unchanging scenery—or it could be a wondrous journey into a mysterious and beautiful land. Wagon trains rolled along gentle country lanes laced with fragrant, colorful wildflowers, sidled along sparkling streams and lakes, camped out beneath the luminous glow of a haunting harvest moon, and gingerly picked their way up mountain paths to glorious vistas. Elizabeth Cummings, traveling in the late 1850s, was awestruck by the mountains of Utah: "Never have I imagined any thing like what I have seen. Do not think me affected when I say my heart ached. It was physical pain produced in me by what I saw.... The most unearthly, weird, wild scenes crowd on my memory."

As they got to know each other, women sought solace and comfort from other women in their wagon trains. They shared companionship as well as trail chores, helped to deliver each other's babies, and nursed one another through illness. They even helped each other go to the bathroom in private; on terrain where no bushes or rocks provided any privacy, women held their skirts out to shield another woman as she relieved herself.

While they washed clothes or sat around the campfire at night catching up on their mending, women confided their hopes and fears to each other. "High teas were not popular," Catherine Haun noted drily, "but tatting, knitting, crocheting, exchanging recepes for cooking beans or dried apples or swap-ping food for the sake of variety kept us in practice of feminine occupations and diversions." The pleasures of such sisterly com-panionship evoked comforting memories of home and more peaceful, orderly times.

Mary Rockwood Powers, another emigrant to California, was forced to say good-bye to her female companions when her husband, a disagreeable sort, had one too many run-ins with their fellow travelers and decided to journey the rest of the way alone with his family. "The women came over to bid me good-bye, for we were to go alone, all alone," Powers wrote in her diary. "There is something peculiar in such a parting on the Plains, one there realizes what a goodbye is. Miss Turner and Mrs. Hendricks were the last to leave, and they bid me adieu the tears running down their sunburnt cheeks. I felt as though my last friends were leaving me, for what—as I thought then—was a Maniac."

This 1854 painting shows three generations of a family moving west. Extended families often traveled together so that they could settle near one another.

Although women usually sought out other women for companionship on the trail, men and women also socialized together, especially at night after they had finished preparing for the next day's journey. Settlers brought along fiddles, guitars, harmonicas, and melodeons, and held impromptu concerts, sing-alongs, and dances around the campfire. Catherine Haun recalled how special these nighttime funfests were, "the menfolk lolling and smoking their pipes and guessing or maybe betting how many miles we had covered the day. We listened to readings, story telling, music and songs and the day often ended in laughter and merrymaking."

In many respects, children's experiences on the trail mirrored those of their parents. Although they did not shoulder nearly as heavy a workload as their elders, they faced the same discomforts of the trail—the harsh weather, long, tedious days

of travel, boring meals. Nor were they shielded from the more severe hardships of travel, especially the reality of death. Children became all too familiar with the painful customs surrounding death. When her baby brother, George, died of dysentery, 12-year-old Ada Millington described in her diary how the family "all gathered around his little bed in the tent to see him die." They even took George's body with them, she explained, because "we couldn't bear the thought of leaving his little body among the sands of this wilderness surrounded by Indians and wolves....We used spirits of camphor very freely on George's clothes and think we will try to take his body on at least another day."

But life on the Overland Trail was far from being dull or sad all of the time. For children as well as for adults, the trail offered adventure, a chance to see new places, and freedom. Young people gathered around the campfire at night to while away the time. Helen Clark, who traveled with her parents from Illinois in 1860, enjoyed nightly dances and music fests around the campfire. While her mother had "a foreboding something is going to happen," Helen was having too good a time to worry about the future. One night her mother had a headache and "is trying to be real [sick] but I hear music in another tent."

Girls and young women like Helen Clark found a freedom on the trail they did not have at home. They got to drive the oxen and spend unchaperoned time with boys. But young women's freedom often ran aground of their mothers' disapproval. During her family's trip to Oregon, Adrietta Hixon confided in her diary, "Mother was always reminding Louvina [her sister] and me to be ladies, but sometimes it seemed to me that the requirements were too rigid, for I also liked to run, jump and climb." Eighteen-year-old Mollie Dorsey Sanford reveled in the freedom and openness of the frontier. When her family moved to Nebraska in 1857, she exulted in her diary, "I already love the Nebraska prairies.... To me, it seems a glorious holiday, a freedom from restraint, and I believe it will be a blessing to we girls."

Although women became fast friends on the trail, there were no guarantees that they would finish the journey together, as Mary Rockwood Powers's experience demonstrated. Wagon trains were impermanent, fractious traveling communities. Even families had to split up. Three generations of John and Jannet Stewart's family—John and Jannet, their five daughters and two sons-in-law, and fourteen grandchildren—left Pennsylvania in 1853 bound for Oregon. One daughter and son-in-law and their eleven children fell behind in Missouri when their wagon broke down and needed repair. The men in the caravan decided to continue on, thinking the stragglers would catch up later that day. But somehow, they kept missing the rest of the family. Not until a year later did the divided family communicate by letter. Elizabeth Stewart Warner, one of Jannet Stewart's daughters, described her mother's anguish. After recounting the men's unilateral decision to push on without waiting for the stragglers, she wrote, "Our wemen protested against it but they started and we were obliged to fowlow.... I do not think that Mother will ever get over it she blames her self for not standing still and she

The members of a wagon train stop in Colorado to pose for a portrait. Women traveling together sought out each other for companionship and support during the long, difficult journey.

blames us for not doing the same and she blames the men for leaving them."

But Jannet Stewart and her family and thousands of other migrants eventually reached their destinations in the West, and soon they faced a whole new set of challenges. They confronted the daunting task of making new homes and building new lives out of the precious but elusive resources of the land. Against the windblown mesas of the desert Southwest, on the prairie grasslands of the Dakotas, in the verdant river valleys of Oregon, and the gold-laced hills of California they staked their claims to their quarter sections and to a future burnished with dreams of wealth and opportunity for themselves and their children.

CHAPTER 4

"SHE WAS A NEAT AND EFFICIENT HOUSEWIFE"

HOMEMAKING ON THE FRONTIER

In 1907, Edith Ammons and her sister, Ida Mary, journeyed first by train and then steamer from St. Louis, Missouri, to the land claim they had made—sight unseen—in the central region of what is now South Dakota. Although they traveled by train and steamship rather than by covered wagon, the journey was still an ordeal. Edith was struck by typhoid fever, and her recuperation delayed their journey by ten days, compounding their already mounting anxiety that someone else would snatch their claim. At last they reached Pierre, the nearest "city" to their claim, and spent the night at a crude, fly-infested hotel. The next morning they set out in a jouncing wagon over the dusty prairies. By the time they reached the claim, they were tired, dirty, and parched with thirst, for there had been no water along the way. All they wanted was to wash off the dust and crawl into a clean, comfortable bed.

But they took one look at their new "home"—and promptly wanted to turn around and go back. "One panic-stricken look at the black tar-papered shack, standing alone in that barren expanse," wrote Edith Ammons later, "and the last spark of our dwindling enthusiasm for homesteading was snuffed out." Timidly they got out of the wagon, paid the driver for his

Despite the rigors of making a home on the frontier, some, like this Colorado woman, faced the task with spunk and determination.

trouble, stepped over the threshold of the shack, ate a cold dinner in the dark, and went to bed, vowing they'd start for home the next day. Instead, they gradually became attached to the land and decided to stay in the West, making a home for themselves in the burgeoning community.

The Ammons sisters were lucky: at least they had a shack, however crude, to live in while they improved their land. Many homesteaders did not even have that basic a home when they arrived at their final destination. As they neared the end of the long journey west, settlers anxiously wondered what new challenges and hardships awaited them. Toward the end of her journey, Katherine Kirk, another homesteader bound for South Dakota, nervously wrote in her diary, "With a sinking feeling I realized that I was entering a new kind of life, as rough and full of ups and downs as the road over which we traveled. Would I have the courage and fortitude to stick it out?"

Other women were eager to establish a permanent home, one more comfortable than the cramped wagons or ship quarters that had been their homes for many months. Anna Goodell simply wanted to "sit at a table and eat like folks and sleep in a house on a bedstead."

Most immigrants arrived at their destinations without furniture or dishes because they had had to discard them along the way—only to discover that their new homes consisted of tumbledown log cabins with no doors or windows, frame and tarpaper shacks with dirt floors and canvas ceilings, soddies made out of hard-packed dirt bricks, or nothing at all. One young 17-year-old bride glared at her mud roof and dirt floor and declared, "My father had a much better house for his hogs."

Rachel Bella Calof, newly arrived on the North Dakota plains after a long journey from Russia to New York City, lived in a pit scooped out of the center of the dirt floor of her in-laws' shack. "Looking about at the people and the space provided for our living," she said, "I knew that I was very close to the living level of an animal."

Of all the various structures that settlers lived in, the tightly packed mud bricks of a soddie—so-called because the

Although soddies—shelters made from tightly packed mud bricks—offered settlers protection from the cold, their dirt walls also provided comfortable homes for a variety of bugs and snakes.

shelter was made from sod, or dirt, instead of wood or clay brick—provided the most protection from the cold; but the dirt walls and ceilings served as a comfortable home for bugs and snakes. "We were kept awake so much by fleas & bed bugs," wrote Myrtle Hopper, who lived in a soddie, "that first thing after breakfast was to tear everything up & clean them well." Many settlers awoke in their soddies only to find a rattlesnake contentedly curled at the foot of their beds or on the floor. Even in wooden structures, rattlers were an unwelcome intrusion. Elizabeth Corey, a vivacious young woman who lived in a wooden shack on her claim near Pierre, South Dakota, wrote her mother, "Say! my quarter is a regular rattlesnake den—its nothing to kill half a dozen in crossing it. You wouldn't catch me any where near there with out a snake stick."

Settlers who did not have homes to move into lived in their wagons or tents or anything else they found until they could build a structure. The 12 members of the Martin and Neher families, who immigrated to America from Russia, spent their first winter in North Dakota in 1909 in an empty boxcar. Fred Martin, one of the two fathers, recalled the horror of living in such a cramped space: "We were crowded together like coyotes and their young in a hole. You can imagine [my daughter] Lena's turmoil: she was in her adolescence, with no privacy whatever, and we did not even recognize a girl's needs…. Lena went through a hard time in her growing up years."

For several winters in a row, Rachel Bella Calof shared her 12-by-14-foot shack not only with her three in-laws but also with assorted cows and chickens because the two families lacked the fuel to heat two separate households during the long, bitterly cold winters. Calof and her husband had to seek their privacy on the open prairie. "Of all the privations I knew as a homesteader," she said later, "the lack of privacy was the hardest to bear."

Just as they embarked on the Overland Trail with little practical knowledge of yoking oxen or scouting out campsites, settlers set about building homes with little know-how. Johnaphene Faulkner described how her two young uncles, who knew nothing about building a house, tried to build a cabin. They managed to get all four walls up—only to discover they had left no openings for doors or windows.

Where they settled often determined what kind of houses settlers built. In the Southwest, Hispanic families often took over Indian dwellings or built temporary jacales of brush and mud. They also constructed dwellings out of adobe, using stretched rawhide for doors and peeled poles for roof beams.

In parts of Texas, settlers built "pole houses" out of limbs stuck into the ground, with moss and grass stuffed in between

Houses made of adobe were common throughout much of the Southwest. Adobe, sundried brick made from native clays and grass or straw, can be very durable as long as no moisture reaches it.

to fill in the cracks. On the plains, houses made out of stacks of baled hay or soddies were common. And where there was timber, settlers constructed their homes out of wood.

Settlers were remarkably resourceful: Ella Bird Dumont and her husband spent a winter in the Texas Panhandle in a house insulated by dried buffalo hides hung up around the walls. She was proud of her house, declaring, "a more clean and comfortable little home you could not find in any of the Eastern cities."

Families who moved to frontier towns often "boarded out" or rented rooms in other homes. Margaret Murray and her family lived in two upstairs rooms. "In our large room," she wrote, "we cooked, ate, & sat. [I carried] our water from a well in the back yard & washed down stains in land ladies kitchen same day she did."

Most boarders were eager to have their own homes. But new construction was expensive, and single-family dwellings were hard to find. Some pioneers bought prefabricated houses in the East and shipped them out West. When settlers finally did have their own homes, they often converted them into a store as well as a house. "We have bought us a house, at last," Sarah Hively exulted. "Paid two hundred and fifty dollars for it. We intend to keep cigar store in the front part and live in the back room."

Even in well-settled cities, settlers lived in cramped, primitive conditions when they could not afford anything better or when racial discrimination prevented them from living elsewhere. In turn-of-the-century El Paso, Texas, Hispanic residents were crowded into the worst slums, without running water, paved streets, electricity, or sewers—urban amenities to which white residents were already accustomed. Anglo property owners refused to pay taxes to finance these services, and the city also refused to furnish them. Consequently, Hispanic women hauled water from the river in buckets, ground corn by hand, and chopped wood for fuel. Because of these poor living conditions, both children and adults suffered from disease and malnutrition.

Twenty years later, conditions in San Francisco were not much better for Chinese residents. Low Shee Law, who migrated to San Francisco in 1922, recalled living in a one-room tenement apartment. She and her husband "did everything in that one room—sit, sleep, and eat. We had a small three-ring burner for cooking, no ice box, and no hot water. We would hand-wash our clothes and dry them on the roof or in the hallways. Those were poor times and it was the same for all my neighbors."

With the same grit and resourcefulness that brought them to the West, women made do with inadequate materials, devising their own household implements and decorative touches. Rachel Bella Calof discovered that her in-laws had no fuel or candles to light their shack at night. Instead, they simply went to bed at sunset. Calof balked at going to bed so early and solved the problem by molding a dish out of partly dried mud, fashioning a wick out of a rag, smearing it with butter for lighter fuel, and lighting the rag wick. Not only did they have light in the shack, they also had ceremonial candles for celebrating the Jewish Sabbath every Friday evening.

Sarah Hartman recalled that her mother made mirrors by stretching an old black shawl over a board and placing a pane of "some of the presious window glass" in front of the shawl. Mrs. Dan Bain of Oklahoma remembered, "I had 58 yards of new rag carpet and we used that to put up around the walls on the inside of the house to make it more comfortable in the wintertime....We used dry goods boxes for a cupboard & for a bureau, and used newspapers for window curtains." With ingenuity and resourcefulness, they found ways to make their rough-hewn shelters cozy and homey, and proudly displayed their good china and other treasures brought from home.

With time, as their incomes improved, families built better homes or enlarged their existing homes by adding an extra room or expanding the kitchen. Mary Annetta Coleman Pomeroy, who emigrated from Utah to Arizona, recalled her joy when she and her husband and child moved out of her in-laws' granary—"which was half full of wheat"—into their own two-room house, furnished with items that her husband bought after selling his cattle. "The house was white-washed and curtains were put up. I was never so happy in my life. I sat in the rocker, listening to the clock tick and watching the baby play on the floor and thought I should burst with pride. We were surely blessed!"

For women, the challenge of making a home in the wilderness shaped their daily lives. Married women, especially those with children, strove to create safe, healthy homes for their families under primitive conditions. They also helped with chores around their farms or ranches. Single or widowed women had the added burden of doing all of the work themselves if no men were available to help them. Most women took comfort from cooking, cleaning, and other household duties, even under such trying conditions, because these tasks had given meaning to their lives back home. As on the trail, their days continued to be a round of cooking, sewing, mending, cleaning, and watching their children, as well as helping out on their claims.

Because there were few, if any, stores nearby, and primitive, unreliable transportation brought little in the way of ready-made goods such as canned foods or clothing, women also performed tasks that were no longer necessary in their former homes. They made their families' clothing and linens, churned butter and made cheese, produced soap and candles, often raised chickens, planted vegetable gardens, and gathered wild herbs and fruits such as currants, cherries, and strawberries. Many also spun yarn and wove cloth, preserved jams and jellies, and cured meat.

Their work was tedious and time-consuming. Matilda Peitzke Paul described the task of churning butter: "The milk was put in pans to cool and left long enough for the cream to come to the top which was about 24 hours, then the cream was skimmed off with this kind of skimmer and kept in a cool place if there was one, until there was enough cream to make several pounds of butter in a dash churn.... I remember how I used to dread to have mother call me and tell me to help with the churning. It seemed as if the butter never would come [since] sometimes it did take for hours to churn."

The lack of nearby stores forced women on the frontier to produce much of the food, including butter, that their families consumed.

Cooking consumed most of women's time. Few frontier families had cookstoves when they first arrived. The large metal stoves they used back home were too heavy to carry out West, and they usually discarded the small camp stoves they had used on the trail. As a result, most women began frontier housekeeping by cooking in an open fireplace or over an outdoor campfire. For women who took pride in their cooking, making meals under these conditions was miserable. Guadalupe Callan recalled how her mother burst into tears after seeing the outdoor campfire that was to be her stove. She fled into the cabin and "picked up an ostrich fan, a relic of past grandeur, and fanned herself," leaving to her daughter the task of cooking dinner.

Settlers improvised iceboxes by storing their food in a hole in the ground. Ada Mae Brinton of Iowa recalled that in the 1910s her husband dug a hole 10 feet deep in the basement floor and lined it with cement. They retrieved their food by a small dumbwaiter operated by a chain and pulley. Amelia

Murdock Wing, also of Iowa, noted that her family stored everything from homemade sauerkraut and canned fruit to milk, cream, and butter in their cellar. "No one had ice in those days, but our cellar was cool."

Because today's bounty could quickly become tomorrow's subsistence when unforeseen natural disasters struck, settlers wasted no scrap of food: chicken meat, for example, was used for the main course; the bones and marrow for soup; and the feathers for bed ticking. Corn "tops and shucks" were also used in soup stock and for ticking. Leftover cake scraps added to water became a sponge starter for bread, and bread crumbs, in turn, became the basis for a dessert crust. Settlers used stale vegetables in soup stock or fried them into fritters. Women learned to make coffee out of browned wheat or roasted corn, baked "vinegar" pies—vinegar substituted for lemon—converted watermelon syrup into sugar, and competed with one another to make the best cakes without butter or eggs. Animal bladders, after being preserved in brine, cleaned, and stretched, became dandy sausage skins. Even discarded potatoes were useful. After roasting them, Mrs. Jared Skinner distributed them to neighboring children during winter to use as hand warmers as they walked to school.

Women, understandably, took pride in turning scraps into a full-course meal. Kitturah Belknap of Iowa once served the following menu for a Christmas dinner for 12 people: "Firstly, for bread, nice light rolls; cake, doughnuts; for pie, pumpkin; preserves, crab apples and wild plums; sauce, dried apples; meat first round; roast spare ribs with sausage and mashed potatoes and plain gravy; second round: chicken stewed with the best of gravy; chicken stuffed and roasted in the Dutch oven by the fire."

Next to cooking, washing clothes was the most frequent chore women performed. Whether they lived on the prairies or in the desert, running water was unheard of. As late as 1935, a survey of six South Dakota counties, selected to be representative of farming areas across the state, revealed that three-fourths of the homes still did not have indoor plumbing, even though plumbing had become readily available in urban areas by 1915. Settlers hauled water from ponds and creeks anywhere from a few feet to a few miles away. Some women found that hauling water consumed most of their days.

But before women could even begin to wash, they had to make soap, a smelly, disagreeable task. Some women purchased lye to use for making soap, but others made the lye themselves by pouring water and lime through ashes saved from the fireplace. They combined the lye with leftover household grease, and boiled the mixture over an open fire until the soap started to thicken. Alice Lund recalled how critical and laborious this stage was: "When the soap started to thicken the kettle had to be watched very closely or it would boil over. When the soap had been cooked enough, it was stirred over and over again. It was beaten until it became white. The more it was beaten the more white the soap became."

Women usually performed this task outdoors, with ashes flying in their faces and the pungent smell of the lye burning their nostrils. After the soap was beaten enough, it was poured into kegs or crocks and left to harden, which usually took one or two days. Then it was cut into bars and stored for use. Or, women used the soap immediately in its brown softened form.

Now the "real" work of clothes washing began. For this task, women needed a tub, scrub board, and batting stick. They sorted the clothes by color and amount of dirt, soaking the dirtiest and boiling the white clothes over a fire. Every garment was scrubbed against the washboard, and the most soiled beaten with the stick to loosen the dirt, then rinsed, wrung out, and starched where necessary, and hung to dry. After that, out came the heavy, solid-iron flatirons to press out everything, including sheets. Women heated several irons at once in the fireplace or on the stove, and as one iron cooled it was quickly exchanged for a hotter one. The ruffles, tucks, fluting, and pleats that ornamented their dresses had to be ironed with special care. No wonder so many women counted laundry as their most detestable chore!

Other time-consuming chores included making candles, washing newly sheared fleece and spinning it into yarn, weaving cloth, and sewing. By the 1880s, many frontier homes had a foot-operated sewing machine, which freed women from doing tedious hand stitching. Most women made at least one good dress to wear for special occasions—weddings, funerals, holiday gatherings. These fancy dresses were usually made out of a rich, heavy silk with layers of lining, crinoline, and boning. Women also sewed dresses for their daughters and jeans and cotton shirts for the men and boys in their family. They knitted warm stockings, mittens, and mufflers, and fashioned hats from straw or wild grasses that they picked from the fields.

Most of the sewing and knitting was done at night, by the light of the fireplace or by a saucer lamp, which was a saucer filled with grease and a piece of twisted rag inserted to serve as a wick. Recalled Margaret Murray: "Mother did all her sewing and knitting by that [saucer lamp] and the light from the fireplace and she sure had a lot of it to do."

Eventually, grocers opened up shops on the frontier, and dry goods merchants sold cloth and yarn. By 1844, Dubuque's Iowa *Territorial Gazette and Advertiser* carried advertisements for

Spinning newly sheared fleece into yarn to use for clothing and linens was one of many arduous tasks that women on the frontier performed for their families.

103

"Hats, Hats," a "Fashionable Milliner and Dress Maker," and "Rich Fancy Goods." Stores in larger settlements advertised silk gloves, kid gloves, linens, boots and shoes, black silk lace edging, as well as patterns for making dresses. Alice L. Longley, an Iowa homesteader in the mid-1850s, bought not only calico and gingham for her everyday dresses but also velvet ribbon, a silk apron, an afternoon tea dress, a fan and parasol, a pair of kid gloves, and yards of lace. Women also subscribed to fashion magazines such as *Godey's Lady's Book*, which offered a mail-order shopping service for braids, laces, and other ornaments not easily found at frontier outposts.

Popular magazines such as Godey's Lady's Book *offered frontier women a chance to order the latest fashions, such as this dress featured in the January 1864 issue.*

For everyday wear, women donned sturdy calico dresses or even bloomers. Miriam Davis Colt, of Kansas, found bloomers "well suited to a wild life like mine. Can bound over the prairies like an antelope, and am not in so much danger of setting my clothes on fire while cooking when these prairie winds blow." But for church, holidays, and other special occasions, people put on their Sunday best. Alice Lund recalled how her neighbors loved to dress for church: "The ladies wore full skirts, over-skirts and hoop-skirts; the men wore long coats with a slit in the back." The hardships of frontier life did not snuff out women's sense of style or desire to look fashionable. As Harriet Carr wrote from Kansas in 1858, "People [out here] are generally...not half so heathenish as many imagine."

The frontier lives of married women also included helping their husbands with the heavy labor of maintaining a farm or ranch. When no other men or boys were available, women helped with the plowing, planting, and harvesting. Women dug cellars, butchered hogs, built cabins, and roped and branded cattle. They learned how to chop wood, drive reapers, and herd sheep. Men did most of the heavy physical labor, while women managed the home and family—but a woman's role as household manager thrust her into nontraditional tasks when necessary to help her family survive. Sarah Kenyon helped her husband reap wheat until he hired a man to help. She looked forward to a respite from the hard physical work, but when the hired hand quit before the fall corn harvest she "shouldered my hoe and have worked out ever since.… I wore a dress with my sunbonnet wrung out in water every few minutes and my dress also wet." Barbara E. Gannon Baker managed to get in a little domestic work while she herded cattle: "I often took my knitting or some other hand work along with me."

Even young girls helped out in the fields. Lily Casey, the daughter of farmers and ranchers in New Mexico, learned to "ride, rope, brand, and perform the various functions of a cowboy." She was also responsible for caring for the Caseys' cattle. Because her parents had only one son, Rosalía Salazar Whelan and her sisters, the daughters of two Sonora Indians who owned a cattle ranch and farm in the Aravaipa Canyon of Arizona, did heavy farm chores as well as the traditional female tasks of washing and ironing. They had to get up before dawn to gather kindling for the morning fire and milk the cows before they went to school. They also picked fruit and vegetables in the fields and did washing and ironing for Anglos to earn extra money. "There were times when I would iron from seven o'clock in the morning until five o'clock in the afternoon," recalled Whelan.

Era Bell Thompson, a young African-American woman who grew up on a farm in south-central North Dakota during the 1910s, loved haying time because the whole family worked together. Her first job was to drive the stacker horse, "one so slow he would have stopped at the stake if I hadn't pulled on the reins." Her next job was to drive the hayrack, a frame mounted on a wagon to haul hay. Years later, she still remembered the special magic of returning home from a day spent in the fields: "The coming-home on a load of hay in the warm silence of twilight—the slow rhythm of tired horses, the muffled rattle of the harness on those tied behind, the hayrack creaking under its burden as we moved slowly across the prairie in the shallow road…had a sacredness about it that filled us with the inner happiness that comes of a day's work well done."

When husbands were disabled by accident or illness, or were away on business, women took over the work of running the farm or ranch. Hilda Rose of Montana almost singlehandedly ran the farm that she shared with her elderly husband and young son. She did all of the planting and plowing, milked the cows and raised the chickens, worried about keeping her family fed and clothed when they had no money, and did all of the other heavy farm chores.

Indeed, some women even preferred "men's" work to household chores. Carrie Dunn said of her mother, "She was a neat and efficient housewife, but repairing fences, searching for livestock or hunting were always legitimate excuses to take her out." And Hilda Rose claimed, "I'd take up a homestead [again] before I'd live in a city. The country has got into my very bones. I love it—the trees and birds and growing things. And city, what would that give me? A little comfort and starve my soul. Better to die fasting with a flower in my hand."

Women were understandably proud of their ranching and farming skills. Boasted Rachel W. Bash: "I was said to be a good

Many women in the West took pleasure in working in the fields, doing tasks that had traditionally been thought of as men's work.

driver of horses. At any rate, when in my buckboard, my husband who was on horseback, unless I wanted him to, could not
pass me." Elinore Pruitt Stewart of Wyoming thrived on the
variety and challenge of ranch work. She raised potatoes, car-
rots, beets, turnips, and more; experimented with a new kind of
squash and successfully grew beans despite her neighbors'
warnings that the climate and soil were not hospitable to them;
raised chickens and turkeys; "milked ten cows twice a day all
summer"; and worked in the fields. "I have tried every kind of
work this ranch affords, and I can do any of it," she wrote. "I
just love to experiment, to work, and to prove out things, so
ranch life and 'roughing it' just suit me."

Besides caring for the house and working around the farm
or ranch, women also sold the products of their labor. Margaret
Murray recalled that her mother "sold Butter, Eggs & Beeswax &
anything we could spare off the farm, [and] in the summer and
fall we gathered Black Berries, wild grapes & anything we raised
on the farm that would bring money or exchange for groceries."
Butter was always in demand in frontier settlements. Women
sold their butter locally or shipped it to more distant markets,
earning 10 to 30 cents per pound for as much as 50 to 100
pounds produced a week.

The ordinary challenges of life on the frontier were
punctuated by days of fear and crisis. Even long after their
homes were established, settlers had to contend with bitter
cold winters, summer droughts, and destructive fires, along
with poverty, violence, and death. Winter nights on the plains
could be terrifying. Edith Ammons described the misery of
weathering a blizzard in a flimsy tarpaper shack: "When
blizzards raged they drove the snow through the shack like
needles of steel. There was not a spot where I could put that
cot to keep dry, so I covered my face with the blankets, which in
the morning were drifted over with snow." She and her sister
once stayed awake all night for fear of freezing to death if they
fell asleep.

Lucy Goldthorpe of Williams County, North Dakota,
endured the bitter winter of 1906–7 all alone in her small

Mrs. Finetta Lord of Montana stands over an animal she has shot. The harsh realities of life on the frontier often required women to hunt for their own food.

shack. Many nights that winter the temperature dropped to 40 degrees below zero. She slept with the few precious vegetables she had to prevent them from freezing and stored her other food and her alarm clock in her oven. "Alone in my homesteader's shack," she said later, "thoughts of freezing to death didn't make my situation any better, so I would make an effort to recall the fun times when I was a youngster."

Prairie fires were a settler's worst nightmare, for most frontier settlements did not have the resources to fight them. In a flash, fires destroyed homes and farms and years of hard work. As if taunting settlers, flames leapt across ditches and roared over open grassland, pulling burning tumbleweed from the soil and pitching it across the cracked earth, spreading flames everywhere. During a fire, Edith and Ida Mary Ammons lost their shack, their supply store, print shop, and post office—the fruits of many years of saving and scrimping to build up a liveli-hood—in a matter of minutes.

Nature sent bizarre plagues as well. Melissa Genett Moore recalled a sudden invasion of grasshoppers on the Kansas prairies. "On one bright, sunshiny afternoon we noticed that the sun was growing dim, and found that the air as high as we could see was alive with flying insects coming nearer and nearer to the ground. Before we could think, grasshoppers were devouring everything green. I looked out at my fine cabbage patch, all nicely headed out—only the bare stalks remained. After they had eaten everything in sight, the grasshoppers did have the good manners to rise and fly away." When the grasshoppers returned a second time, they "deposited immense numbers of eggs in every acre of cultivated land. Corn planted the next spring got a few inches high when the grasshoppers began to hatch, and they soon made away with it."

Summer droughts were just as treacherous. Anna Langhorne Waltz of South Dakota nearly went insane with des-peration during a drought. While carrying her water can up from her cellar, she accidentally spilled the last drops of water left for her thirsty baby. After two days of bearing her baby's cries of misery, she panicked and ran out into the blistering hot canyons around her soddie, to look for water. "The last thing I remembered, I was pulling at my hair and running.... My lips were cracking." Sometime later, other settlers found her "exhausted and in a daze," wandering through the broiling scrubland. They took her back to her soddie and nursed her and her baby back to health.

Poverty compounded the hardships of frontier life. Korean immigrant Mary Paik was eleven when her family was forced to ration food in order to survive. At the time, they were living in the small northern California town of Colusa. Mary, her father, and her brothers and sisters could find no work because of a floundering local economy—and because the town's racist citi-zens would not hire Koreans for the few jobs available. "After paying the rent, light, water, and other bills, we had very little left over for food," said Mary Paik. "Mother made tiny biscuits each morning and served one biscuit and a tin cup of water to each of us three times a day. During the time we lived in Colusa, we had no rice, meat, or anything besides biscuits to eat."

Infant mortality rates on the frontier were high—as much as 25 to 30 percent of all births—because of the crude, unsanitary conditions and because mothers were not always in the best of health when they gave birth, owing to poor diets and overwork. Mrs. William Poston confided mournfully to her diary, "I feel perfectly careless and indifferent. My Babes all snatched from me one by one. [I]t is hard to bear."

Some women became so discouraged or depressed from the hardships that they just gave up. Some committed suicide; others, like Abigail Malick's daughter, went insane or were so paralyzed by depression that they were committed to institutions. Anna Pike Greenwood of Idaho described how her neighbor, Mrs. Howe, simply lost her will to live on the frontier. When she first arrived in Idaho, said Greenwood, Mrs. Howe was "beautiful, with dark eyes, rosy cheeks, and a great rope of chestnut hair wound in a coronet around her head." Though she brought with her books and fine furniture and "one of the most modern of phonographs," she and her husband and five children soon sunk to "a state lower than the farm animals." They had succumbed to the rigors of frontier life. Also, noted Greenwood, "the father had the beating habit."

Greenwood's neighbor took to her bed and stayed there. She was physically ill and so dispirited that she just gave up on life. When Greenwood and two other women went to see her, they were appalled. "I was shocked," recalled Greenwood. "That glorious hair was a solid, dingy, repulsive mat on her head. It could not have been washed or combed for months. We women dared not cut it off, for we had not the right, but that is what would have to be done with it. As Miss Butterworth turned back the covers to bathe her, there scurried across the grimy undersheet literally scores of big dark-red bedbugs. They had been feeding on the helpless sick woman."

The women changed her soiled bed linen, fed her homemade rolls, roasted chicken, and delicate custard, and arranged to have her committed to a sanitarium. "My friend had almost totally lost her mind," wrote Greenwood. In the sanitarium, she recovered enough to enjoy "sitting there," but she "yearned not at all for the tar-paper shack, her five children, or her husband."

Women who were committed to institutions for depression brought on by isolation were called "prairie women." Before 1870, there were three insane asylums in the Northwest: one in Stockton, California, and one each in Salem and Portland, Oregon. Records for the asylum in Portland showed that at first the ratio of female to male patients was one to three, but within ten years, the number of female patients had risen to one half.

Some women finally had enough and simply refused to endure any more hardship or upheaval. Rena Matthews of California recalled that her mother "followed her husband, with a growing family of five, from one end of the state to another.... After seventeen years of these wanderings, Mother obtained a separation and settled in Sacramento."

But other women began to find their peace and pleasure in the spacious realms of the West. Despite their determination to return to their former home, Edith and Ida Mary Ammons discovered that the Dakota prairies had become their home. "Imperceptively we had come to identify ourselves with the West," wrote Edith. "We were a part of its life, it was a part of us. Its hardships were more than compensated for by its unshackled freedom. There was a pleasant glow of possession in knowing that the land beneath our feet was ours."

CHAPTER 5

"I WAS FULL OF MY DUTIES AND MY PLEASURES"

MAKING A LIFE ON THE FRONTIER

I n 1896, Mary Anderson and her friend Bee Randolph homesteaded adjoining quarter sections and shared a shack built over the property line. When Mary was married a year later, Bee wrote sadly, "Dear Mame—Here we are in our little preemption home for the last time together, at least for some year to come. But I hope sometime we may visit it again. We cannot be happier than we have been here, although we may have wealth and other great pleasures. Can you not almost remember every day from the first, what has happened? Our laughing, singing, playing, working, our company, etc."

Many women homesteaders were not as fortunate as Bee Randolph and Mary Anderson. They settled into their new homes with few, if any, neighbors nearby. In some areas, there were as many as six men for every woman. Mollie Dorsey Sanford, who settled in Nebraska, confided to her diary, "I do try to feel that it is all for the best to be away off here.... If the country would only fill up....We do not see a woman at all. All men, single or bachelors, and one gets tired of them."

Even frontier cities were almost devoid of women. In the 1850s, Elizabeth Minerva Byers wrote, "I was the 8th white woman in Denver." And in San Francisco, Mary Pratt Staples

Two women in Helena, Montana, pause to chat on the streets of their rapidly expanding new town.

observed, "Men were to be seen everywhere, nothing but men, not a woman—nor a child." The scarcity of women meant they were often treated as honored guests. In California, a 17-year-old New England boy once rode 35 miles, after working all week in his father's claim, because he wanted to see a miner's wife who had come to a nearby camp. "I wanted to see a home-like lady; and, father, do you know, she sewed a button on for me, and told me not to gamble and not to drink. It sounded just like mother."

Even married women longed for company. Husbands were no substitutes for female friends, especially when the men were away from home so much, hunting and fishing, driving stock to market, or going for supplies. Men had more opportunities to socialize than married women. Susan E. Newcomb of Texas observed that "a woman does not see much satisfaction in this country. There husbands are never with them much.... The men are always with a croud, they see people nearly everyday. They hear news while they are gone and they are gone so long that they forget it before they get home." She complained that her own husband was down at the local store playing checkers too many nights. "It seems to me that he would rather be their playing them than to be at home with me and his little boy.... I don't guess that he is thinking or caring how long and lonesome the hours are to me here alone in this old cabin."

In San Francisco's Chinatown, the small number of Chinese women who came to America to join their husbands in the late 19th century remained sequestered at home, just as they had been in China. Compounding these restrictive cultural traditions were the alienation and anti-Chinese hostility they encountered in this strange new land. Because they spoke no English, were economically dependent on their husbands, and lived among other Chinese women who were traditional, they continued to be subservient to their husbands. Although many women took in washing and sewing at home, they had little contact with other women workers. In Chinatown, only men could join the clan associations and trade guilds, or organized groups of fellow workers, that made up social life in the district; women had no voice or role in public affairs.

"In China I was shut up in the house since I was 10 years old," one merchant's wife said, "and only left my father's house to be shut up in my husband's house in this great country. For seventeen years I have been in this house without leaving it save on two evenings." She spent her days worshipping at the family altar, doing embroidery, taking care of her son, playing cards with her servants, and visiting with her Chinese neighbors.

Yet Chinese women who were married also found some advantages to living in America. In China, they often lived with their mothers-in-law, who could be tyrants because that was the one position of power for women in China. Or, if their husbands were wealthy, they had to share his attention with a concubine or mistress. But in America, there were no mothers-in-law or mistresses. And because Chinese women were scarce in the New World, and a wife's home-based work was essential to the family's struggle to survive, Chinese husbands valued their wives more than they did in China. However isolated they may have felt in the home, Chinese wives played a vital role in the family economy by taking in sewing or washing. And they were responsible for preserving Chinese cultural traditions and values in the home.

Settler women found a variety of ways to cope with their loneliness and alienation. They pursued activities that reminded them of home. Those who were literate cried and poured out their feelings to their diaries and wrote letters to friends and family back home. In their correspondence, women expressed their craving for news about family and friends, sent swatches of fabric from dresses or linens they were sewing, and in turn eagerly received seeds from former gardens and press clippings from hometown newspapers. But when their letters were not promptly answered, women feared that family or friends had forgotten them, or that some catastrophe had struck. After no word came from her sister for almost a year and a half, Elisabeth Adams of Iowa implored her to write. "Do you not love me?" she wailed. Abigail Malick of Oregon pleaded with her daughter to write. "I fear that Some Thing Serious is the Matter With

Quilting bees, such as this one in Portland, Oregon, offered women a chance to gather together to share news and household hints.

Som of you that you Do not Want us to know About.... O Mary Ann Do Not Forget A Mother that Loves you so Much and Wantes to se you so Much My Dear Child. With tears in My eyes I write this."

Despite the long distances between frontier homesteads, women found ways to socialize. They visited each other's homes, bringing their needlework or knitting to do while their hostess did her chores. They also shared some household tasks, such as making cheese, quilting, and spinning. Kitturah Belknap of Iowa, who hated sorting different grades of wool alone, solved the problem by inviting "about a dozen old ladies in an[d] in a day they will do it all up." Quilting bees drew neighbors from all around the district. As they sat and stitched, women gossiped, shared news and household hints, and sometimes lambasted their husbands.

Cheese making drew husbands as well as wives and children. Because each family did not have enough milk cows for making cheese, they all pooled their fresh milk and gathered at a neighbor's house to make cheese, rotating from house to house until every family had an ample supply of cheese. Recalled Alice Lund: "These gatherings were far from dull, for old and young feasted and had a jolly good time." Settlers turned other household chores into parties as well. Caroline Cock Dunlap of Washington Territory recalled going to ironing parties. "While we ironed the gentlemen prepared supper. They were experts at baking clams, oysters on the half shell and mixing innocent drinks. Thus we turned work into play and obliterated hardship."

Besides helping each other with chores, women organized unofficial welcoming committees to greet newcomers or to assist a neighbor in need. Lois Holman wrote her mother that when she arrived in Sergeant Bluff, Iowa, "the lades have all called on me that live here in the City whitch concists the whole of six." Shortly after Edith and Ida Mary Ammons moved to South Dakota, they looked out across the plains and saw three hardy young women riding in their direction. Their visitors, who lived "only eighteen miles" away, came to welcome the newcomers and stayed on into the night.

Through the cycles of life, from marriage to childbirth and finally death, women comforted and assisted one another. When women were ready to give birth, they wanted other women around them. "A woman that was expecting had to take good care that she had plenty fixed for her neighbors when they got there," commented one frontier woman from Kansas. "There was no telling how long they was in for. There wasn't no paying these friends so you had to treat them good." And when no undertaker was available to prepare the dead for burial, men and women washed and clothed the bodies of the dead.

The members of the Ladies' Imperial Band of Bozeman, Montana. Frontier communities eagerly organized dances, parades, and other musical events where such bands performed.

117

The eagerness for fellowship extended beyond women's friendships and embraced frontier communities. Many families had managed to bring pianos, small organs, or melodeons on the trek west. Others brought violins, fiddles, guitars, and other smaller instruments, and some frontier communities organized local bands to play at dances, parades, and patriotic events.

Later, when school buildings were built, they doubled as social centers for parties, special holiday events, debates, political gatherings, amateur theatricals, recitations, and spelling bees. Margaret Murray of Iowa recalled, "[W]e always in winter time [had] spelling school one night a week at the schoolhouse. Old & young went & all took part it was fun for the children to spell down their parents." Mary Elizabeth Smith of Missouri recalled hearing an astronomy lecture one week and a ballooning lecture the following week.

In the Pacific Northwest, homesteaders enjoyed going clamming together, and throughout the West settlers organized berry and fishing parties. Effie May Butler Wiltbank recalled, "We enjoyed very much…going to the mountains for thorny gooseberries, or down into the canyons along the river for wild grapes…. Soon after the middle of August parties were organized and men, women, and children could be seen heading for the mountain or down the canyon to gather our winter fruit."

"Play-parties" were a form of entertainment unique to the frontier. In settlements where churchgoers disapproved of dancing or where no musicians or musical instruments were available, settlers organized play-parties with the resources at hand. Young men on horseback rode through the region to announce the time and place of a play-party, and at dusk the guests would congregate at the designated spot. The host and hostess cleared out all furniture from the party room and set makeshift benches around the sides of the room. Each guest took his or her turn singing the familiar tunes to which they played games such as Snap, Pig in the Parlor, Bounce Around, and Skip-to-my-Lou. At midnight, everyone stopped to have refreshments, then continued to party until dawn. Play-parties remained popular throughout the late 19th and early 20th

This group gathered to collect nuts in Red Oak, Iowa. Nutting parties, picnics, and other recreational activities helped to ease the hardships of frontier life.

centuries, until more organized forms of entertainment replaced this impromptu form of fun.

Holidays were especially festive when families lived near each other. They improvised to add color and cheer to the occasion. Mothers popped corn and made molasses candy for their children. Families entertained each other or gathered for parties or a play or recitation at the schoolhouse. Ada Mae Brinton recalled her school's special Christmas celebration: "For Christmas there was always a large evergreen tree decorated by tinsel and lights. At the close of the program Santa Claus would appear from the entrance to the auditorium causing great excitement by his costume and chatter. At the time of my earliest recollection presents were hung on the tree. The packages were labeled for the smaller children."

Festive religious traditions offered a brief respite from the hardships of daily life. When Rachel Bella Calof of North Dakota gave birth to a baby boy, she and her family eagerly planned the traditional Jewish celebration of his birth. This celebration marked the biblical covenant that Abraham, patriarch of the Jewish people, made with God in the Old Testament, and was a joyous as well as solemn occasion. Calof and her husband roasted two chickens and served cheese and butter—"a real banquet," she said, compared to their usual meals. "For years there had been little cause for celebration for any of us," Calof explained, "and now it was as though a great yearning to be joyous, to reaffirm that life was worthwhile, was expressed through this festival."

Mary Bernard Aguirre, who settled in New Mexico in 1863, described the pageantry and excitement of the annual feasts held by Hispanic citizens to celebrate their patron saints. At one such feast, she attended high mass, and even sat in front of the altar holding a candle, then attended the bullfight in the church plaza the next day.

Social gatherings and festivities were beacons of gaiety and pleasure in an otherwise harsh existence. From the start, daily life was a struggle to survive—and often remained hard for years to come. Nature was the settlers' friend when gentle rain-showers brought much-needed water for crops, but the enemy when the earth was dry as a tinderbox or was buried under a swirling blizzard.

Nature controlled the settlers' lives. Many marriages were strained almost beyond endurance by the struggle to eke out a living. Fred Martin and his wife and children, immigrants from Russia, coped not just with the hardships of the frontier but also with the challenge of adjusting to a brand-new homeland. Martin later marveled at how they had survived the terrible first years on the North Dakota frontier, for his wife, Sophie, "loathed everything about America and never stopped thinking about the Groszliebental life. It is odd we even slept together, but we had no other choice....We were stuck on this prairie and had to endure it and hope it would be kind enough to produce food."

Pauline Diede, whose family came over from Russia with the Martins, claimed that she often found her mother "crying and wonder whether she cried of fatigue, craving a word of recognition, gratitude, or praise"—none of which she ever received from her husband or children. Like that of so many other pioneer women, her day began at dawn and "did not end until the small hours."

Perhaps it was no coincidence that the western states were the most permissive in granting divorces and offered the most simplified divorce procedure. Even in California, where the powerful Catholic Church opposed divorce, an annulment—a legal dissolution of the marriage vows—was generally easy to obtain. In California, as in many states throughout the 19th century, husbands controlled a couple's property. But in California, when couples divorced, women had a legal right to half that property. And if their husbands' actions had caused the divorce, women gained custody of their children.

Yet for every failed or unhappy marriage on the frontier, there were marriages that flourished because both partners worked together to make their homesteading venture succeed. Martín Amador and his wife, Refugio, Hispanic residents of Las Cruces, New Mexico, became one of the region's most prosperous and influential Hispanic families. They came to Las Cruces in the early 1860s from southern Mexico, and embarked upon several farming enterprises. Gradually they expanded their farm holdings and undertook other business ventures. Throughout the 1870s and 1880s, Don Martín owned and operated numerous businesses, and served as a probate judge and U.S. marshal. He was active in the Republican party and sponsored cultural and agricultural reforms in the Mesilla Valley. When he traveled, Doña Refugio managed the family's thriving farm enterprises as well as land that she had inherited from her mother and retained as her own property, a traditional right of Hispanic women. Together, they reared a large family, presided over successful business ventures, and circulated among Las Cruces's most prestigious citizens.

Orrin and Ruth Hall, of Colorado, had a successful wheat crop in 1917. They bought a four-bedroom frame house with indoor plumbing. Ruth longed to enjoy "all this luxury after eight years in the little sod house," but Orrin was in no rush to move; he thought their new quarters should "cure for a while." Ruth disagreed, and she prevailed. "The wildlife could have the soddy," she wrote later. "I was getting out. So we moved into our new house in April 1918." The rigors of making a new life on the frontier could destroy a marriage or foster greater interdependence and respect between husband and wife.

For couples with children, the challenges were even more daunting. During hard times, children suffered as well as parents. Both parents had to be resourceful in finding ways to feed and clothe their families when money was scarce. Melissa Genett Moore remembered that during the winter of 1858–59 on the Kansas frontier, she and her brothers and sisters had no shoes and little hope of getting any. Her mother made do by collecting the men's discarded work boots, ripping, soaking, and pounding them to soften the leather, and refitting them to the children's sizes. "There were no barefooted children in our family that winter, as there were in many other families."

It was no wonder that parents often did not have time for their children—they were simply too busy trying to keep them alive. Pauline Diede of North Dakota recalled that her mother was so busy with farm chores and with the two younger children, who "constantly yelped or whimpered," that she had no time or energy left over for the older children. "I cannot ever remember Ma taking time to hold me.... It seemed so many pioneer mothers had no time, nor patience, nor ability to reason. There was no time to talk or teach, only punish when something went wrong."

Small wonder, too, that women wanted to limit the number of children they bore. As on the trail, childbirth on the frontier could be a harrowing experience because so few doctors were available and women had to rely on neighbors or husbands who had little medical knowledge. Martha Summerhayes, who gave birth to her first child at Camp Apache, Arizona, recalled her own nightmarish experience: "So here I was, inexperienced and helpless, alone in bed, with an infant a few days old.... I struggled along, fighting against odds; how I ever got well at all is a wonder.... I had no advice or help from any one."

But giving birth was only part of the struggle. Keeping newborns alive in the first precarious weeks after birth was another ordeal. Even when doctors were available, their fees were beyond the means of many families, or they were ill-trained and ill-equipped to treat patients. When Rachel and Abraham Calof took their ailing child to a doctor in a town near their North Dakota homestead, he was mystified by the child's deteriorating condition. Calof later said scornfully, "He was typical of the transient frontier doctors of this time who were more qualified to treat pigs than people."

Children who survived infancy were still vulnerable to all kinds of diseases and accidents. Rattlesnakes, centipedes, scorpions, and other poisonous critters preyed upon children and adults alike. As on the trail, young children were prone to wander off and get lost or attacked by wild animals. Even in the confines of the cabin or soddie, children could fall into the fire or get burned by the stove.

The fear of disease was ever present because of the scarcity of medical services on the frontier. "At last we were visited by that terrible Foe, chills and fever," one Iowa woman wrote, "which attacked ourselves and baby Lucien everyday with grim vengeance; and as we had no one to wait upon us, our suffering and loneliness was hard to bear."

Medical books addressed ailments of animals but offered little advice on how to treat snake bites, set broken arms or legs, or care for seriously ill children. Most women relied on simple home remedies, vigilant nursing, and prayer. Their medical cabinets included peppermint, which, according to Effie May Butler Wiltbank, "would cure anything that ailed you—from colic in newborn babes—to aches and pains accompanying old age"; yarrow for coughs, colds, and menstrual cramps; Epsom salts for purgatives; and mustard plasters. Some women also sought medical advice from Native American women who knew how to make healing balms from wild herbs and grasses and guidance from Hispanic *curanderas,* women who served as healers in their communities.

Frontier women tried to prevent childbirth by using birth control and homemade abortifacients. They consulted medical manuals, and used birth control methods such as vaginal sponges, pessaries, condoms, douches that killed sperm, and coitus interruptus. After 1864, a vaginal diaphragm was also available. In Texas, black women used indigo or calomel and turpentine to "unfix" themselves after they became pregnant. "In them days," Lu Lee Cook recalled, "the turpentine was strong and ten or twelve drops would miscarry you."

Some women were desperate to prevent more pregnancies. Among them was Lizzie Neblett. "I know no doom that would horrify me," she wrote her husband on May 24, 1864, "so much as to know or believe that, 12 years to come, could add five more children to my number. I had rather spend the remainder of my life even tho it were 35 years in the Penitentary or in solitary confinement." She urged her husband to obtain some "preventitives" for her. "Let me say right here that if you apply and get your wine detail this summer don't start home without a good quantity of pulverized Ergot and as good a syringe as you can find." But for most women of childbearing age, childbirth was a fact of life. As Rachel Bella Calof ruefully noted, pregnancy was the "most dependable state of affairs" during the many years she lived on the prairie.

What did frontier life hold for the children who came or were born in the West? Like their parents, they were not strangers to hard physical work. When children were young, they shared chores. Both boys and girls learned how to do household tasks, such as cooking and baking, making soap or candles, and spinning, weaving, and knitting. When they turned nine or ten, they also shared chores out in the field—plowing, herding cattle, and carrying wood or water. As children grew, girls often did more household chores while boys performed outdoor tasks. Amanda Gaines commented in her diary, "I assist Mother in house-hold duties which are various. She is preparing me for a Farmer's wife."

But there were exceptions; children worked wherever their labor was needed. Pauline Diede recalled, "Our clan of growing girls were brought up to strict hard work, especially the two eldest, Matilda and Ottilia, who became field workers. They were expected to do as much work as a man...hauling hay and pitching bundles for the threshing machine.... I...was chore girl to help Mother with domestic work." In their new, bigger home "all of us cleared stones from new broken fields and manured barns, part of the hard manual labor that was every-day work for us."

Matilda Peitzke Paul said that before she was old enough to do other field work she often had to fetch water from a spring and carry it out to the fields for the other workers. She also stayed out in the fields to chase blackbirds away from the cornstalks, pulled weeds to feed to the hogs, and helped pick wild strawberries every June. Come threshing time, she helped carry bundles of newly threshed grain stalks for shocking; later on, she also helped bind the grain. And, after harvest and haying was finished, "we had to dig the potatoes and husk the corn ready for winter."

Parents sometimes hired out their children for paid work on other homesteads. When a farmer approached Fred Martin to hire some of his older children for work, Martin agreed—without consulting his wife or children. His word was their command. He didn't even know where the farmer lived or what kind of work he wanted the children to do. As it turned out, the farmer worked Martin's son and daughter like draft animals, badgered and threatened them, and subjected them to inhuman living conditions. Finally, Martin's wife had a premonition that they were in trouble and insisted that they come home.

Some children took pride and pleasure in their farm chores. Adele Orpen, who at age seven immigrated with her father to Kansas in 1862, took over many farm chores when their hired hands went off to fight in the Civil War. Her days flew by in a flurry of activity. At nine, she claimed, she could not spell her

Children began doing chores around the farm at a very early age. Both boys and girls worked out in the fields and did household tasks.

name, but she knew how to find lost cattle. "Was I lonely [on the prairie]? Not a bit of it. I simply did not know what loneliness meant. I was full of my duties and my pleasures. The day was never long enough for me."

Children's experiences on the frontier often depended upon where they lived and their parents' economic situation. Edna Hedges, 11-year-old daughter of a wealthy lawyer and politician in the mining town of Helena, Montana, sewed, dusted, took music lessons and Bible study, held tea parties and played parlor games with friends, and spent time with her parents in genteel pursuits. By contrast, Anne Ellis of Bonanza, Colorado, spent her evenings reading "Peck's Bad Boy" with Lil, a local "notorious woman," and could describe the smells of a saloon ("strong, sickening") and a brothel ("sweet").

But throughout the Wild West all children—whether they lived in mining towns, on ranches or farms, on the desert, or up in the mountains—were exposed to violence and lawlessness. In mining towns, saloons, bordellos, and gambling halls flourished. Children were witnesses to drinking, prostitution, gambling, gunfights, and foul language. The free flow of slang and liquor worried parents who wanted to cultivate genteel manners in their children. "Must my little girl soil her sweet mouth with such words and expressions?" wailed Elizabeth Fisk of Montana. She feared that her daughter could become a "fast western woman." Louise Walters, an Idaho mother, wrote to friends, "This is the hardest place to live upon principle I ever saw, and the young are almost sure to be led away."

Violence and the threat of bodily harm came as close as a family's front door. During a feud between a gunslinger and the editor of the *Rocky Mountain News* in Denver, Colorado, Agnes Miner and the other children from her one-room school were sent to the safety of their homes. There her mother wrapped her and her sister and brother in buffalo robes and tucked them up in the attic to escape any stray bullets during the coming shootout. The young Agnes also watched a man hanged, and she barely escaped being killed in an Indian assault during a trip back to Denver. "We could see the Indians all along the horizon," she later recalled, and "we were expecting never to see the rising sun again." But friends and neighbors on horseback rescued them, and they safely returned home to Denver.

Homesteading was surely not for the fainthearted. The crude living conditions and physical isolation, the fear of Indian attacks, the rampant lawlessness and violence of the frontier, and the yearning for loved ones left behind—any one of these hardships was enough to drive some women back home. For other women, the appeal of the West eclipsed these dangers and hardships. Era Bell Thompson loved autumn best of all on the prairie. "There were quiet, silent days when the grain fields were hills of whispering gold, undulating ever so softly in the bated breeze," she recalled. "So warm, so tranquil was the spell that one stretched out on the brown, dry earth.... The sun alone stood between you and the blue sky of your God. Time stood still."

Hundreds of miles away, on the parched desert sands of Nevada, Ida Meecham Strobridge, who grew up in the desert and returned to ranch and mine for gold, described the elusive magic that kept so many settlers rooted to the land. "If you go to the Desert, and live there, you learn to love it. If you go away, you will never forget it for one instant.... It will be with you in memory forever and forever. And always will you hear the still voice that lures one, calling—and calling."

CHAPTER 6

"I LOVE TO WORK
WITH CATTLE"

WESTERN WOMEN
AT WORK

During her honeymoon in the winter of 1897, Marietta Palmer Wetherill accompanied her husband, Richard, on an expedition into Grand Gulch, Utah, to collect archaeological specimens for the American Museum of Natural History in New York City. He also wanted to document the discovery of the Anasazi Basketmakers, an Indian tribe that lived in the cliffs of New Mexico's Chaco Canyon. Marietta Wetherill was the only woman in a trekking party of 13 men and 68 pack animals—and probably the first Anglo woman to make such a dangerous journey. The trekkers slowly picked their way up the steep cliffs. "It was so crooked that even a rattlesnake would have a hard time getting down without breaking its back," she wrote later. Nine of the horses tumbled down the cliffs to their deaths. At the camp they set up, Wetherill kept records of all the artifacts that her husband and the other explorers brought in. The work days were long, from dawn to darkness, and the temperature was frigid at night. During one snowy night, as they lay in their makeshift bed beneath the ledge of a cave, her husband suddenly said, "Those mummies, they'll get wet." He sprung out of bed and Marietta, nearly asleep, could hear footsteps padding back and forth. Then

One woman ropes a cow while another brands it during a typical day of work on a Kansas ranch.

she heard her husband say, "Where would you like them—at the head of the bed or at the foot?"

Marietta bolted upright, no longer sleepy. Kneeling next to their bedroll was her husband, holding two mummies. Other mummies stood propped up against the wall. He had retrieved all of the mummies from their unprotected campsite. Marietta stared into the shriveled, brown, eyeless faces of several mummies. Finally, she found her voice and said, "At the foot, Mr. Wetherill. At the foot of the bed."

Few women who went west could boast of such exotic adventures or pursue such exciting work. But the West did open up many new employment opportunities for women. It had long been customary for women to turn profits from the products they made at home, such as butter, pies, fruits, and eggs. But by 1900, women throughout the West were also working in a wide range of occupations outside the home, from dressmaking to blacksmithing to banking. Schools and boardinghouses were staffed predominantly by women. And like women back East, some western women became lawyers and doctors.

Many women's businesses grew out of the need for facilities to house and feed western travelers. Luzena Stanley Wilson served as cook and banker for miners in Nevada City, California, during the Gold Rush. "With my own hands I chopped stakes, drove them into the ground, and set up my table. I bought provisions at a neighboring store and when my husband came back at night he found…twenty miners eating at my table. Each man as he rose put a dollar in my hand and said I might count on him as a permanent customer. I called my hotel 'El Dorado.'" Soon she had hired a cook and waiters and "took my husband into partnership."

Wilson also served as a banker for the miners, storing their gold dust for them. "Many a night have I shut my oven door on two milk-pans filled high with bags of gold dust and I have often slept with my mattress lined.... I must have had more than two hundred thousand dollars lying unprotected in my bedroom." Wilson also made high-interest loans.

Mrs. Bilderbeck stands outside the ramshackle board- inghouse she ran for the Globe Boston Mining Company in Arizona.

Boardinghouses headed by women were common features of western towns. Most were small, accommodating eight to ten boarders at a time. But some were also quite large. Cora Belle Mitchell of Colorado claimed that she "took 77 boarders from Wisconsin and Canada." Sometimes husbands and wives went into business together. The women took charge of traditional domestic tasks—cooking, cleaning, washing, and supervising other domestic helpers—and the men handled the finances, entertained customers, and did routine repairs.

Some boardinghouses were little more than tents or other makeshift structures. Mary D. Ballou described the kitchen of her boardinghouse: "All the kitchen that I have is four posts stuck down into the ground and covered over the top with a factory cloth no floor but the ground.... I am scareing the Hogs out of my kitchen and Driving the mules out of my Dining room. You can see by the description of that I have given you of my kitchen that anything can walk into the kitchen that chooses to walk in....there I hear the Hogs in my kitchen turning the Pots and kettles upside down, so I must drop the pen and run and drive them out."

Even with better-equipped kitchens, running a boardinghouse was exhausting work. Mary Jane Megquier, a boardinghouse keeper in San Francisco, described a typical day: At 7:00 A.M., she was preparing the morning meal and supervising the woman who was "sweeping and setting the table." After breakfast, she did the baking, planned and prepared the rest of the day's meals, made the beds, did the washing, and made or mended the sheets, pillowcases, and other linens. "[H]ad I not the constitution of six horses I should [have] been dead long ago but I am going to give up in the fall weather or no as I am sick and tired of work."

Despite the hard work, operating a boardinghouse often gave women considerable status and power. Nellie Cashman, who provided clean beds and the best meals in town in her frontier community, was a local institution. In Helena, Montana, women who owned property or ran boardinghouses and hotels in the 1870s and 1880s controlled as much as 80 percent of the available housing. And in Denver, Colorado, women hotelkeepers as well as other working women were

Mrs. M. J. Gould stands with her staff in front of the hotel that she operated in a small Oklahoma town. Western women wasted no time in turning their domestic skills into successful businesses, such as running boardinghouses and hotels.

actually able to obtain bank loans more easily than men, even when they had no other property or money to pay the lender if they became unable to repay the loan.

While some women operated boardinghouses, other women hired themselves out as cooks and laundresses in these makeshift establishments, or worked as cooks and housekeepers for single men or families. Ann Beisel claimed that she had "cooked in every hotel in Bartlesville [Oklahoma]." Widows and single young women who were supporting their families or who wanted to finance an education held most of these positions.

Wages were slightly higher out West; between 1885 to 1890, working-class women in Boston made approximately $4.91 a week. Nationwide, the average salary of a working-class woman was $5.64 during that same period, but in California working-class women averaged $6.51 a week. In the 1880s and 1890s, domestic servants in California earned between 20 and 30 dollars a month compared to 10 dollars a month in the South. Cultural customs and social discrimination often determined the kind of paid work a woman could do. Chinese women, unaccustomed to venturing out beyond their homes, especially into a strange new land that did not welcome them, usually worked at home. They took in laundry or sewing, or did piecework such as rolling cigars or making slippers or brooms. Women who lived in fishing villages helped bring in the catch and process the fish. Some Chinese immigrant women also helped their husbands operate laundries, restaurants, and stores. Chinese families usually lived above or behind their storefronts.

Eleven-year-old Mary Paik, a Korean immigrant, worked as a domestic servant before and after school and all day Saturdays and Sundays. In the mornings, the young girl helped set the table and prepare breakfast before going to school, washed the dishes, and cleaned the kitchen. After school, she did the same tasks to help prepare for dinner. And on weekends, she hand washed and ironed all of the family's clothes and linens. "By midnight," she said later, "I was so tired I could hardly walk home." For these long hours and many chores, she received only one dollar a week.

Hispanic women were also exploited. Many Hispanic women in the Southwest were the main breadwinners for their families because their husbands, unable to find work in town, had left to seek work elsewhere. As more Anglo settlers arrived and took control of local economies, most of these women had no choice but to work for Anglos as laundresses, domestics, seamstresses, and in other low-paying jobs. They also earned money from plastering and weaving, and from peddling traditional handcrafts and chili peppers. During World War I, more Hispanic women worked as farm laborers to meet the nation's growing demand for food. And by the 1920s, they worked in garment and cigar factories or as clerks, cooks, and dishwashers. But in all of these occupations, they received the lowest wages because they were women and they were Hispanic.

Throughout the West, black women also worked as domestics, laundresses, seamstresses, and midwives because these were usually the only jobs available to them. When a young black woman in Spokane, Washington, applied for a job as a librarian in 1916, the library board turned her down because of her color and was astonished that "a colored girl should presume to ask such a privilege."

But some African-American women overcame racial barriers to create successful businesses. Among the most successful was Mary Ellen Pleasant. Born into slavery, she spent her young adult years in Boston, and married into wealth. In 1849 or 1850, she moved to California, where she opened a series of boardinghouses and watched her wealth grow from investments in mining stocks and high-interest loans she had made. She used her money to help former slaves, find employment for blacks, and contribute to civic and cultural causes. She also

Sybil Harper, a midwife from Lakeview, Oregon. Because few early frontier communities had doctors, midwives were called upon to deliver babies and care for the ill.

successfully sued the city of San Francisco to permit blacks to ride streetcars.

Harriet Owens-Bynum, another black woman, operated a laundry, bakery, and dairy in Los Angeles, and eventually became a successful real estate agent in the 1880s. And throughout the West, a number of black women opened up beauty parlors and cosmetic businesses for both black and white women. In fact, for a long time, the only hair salon in Carson City, Nevada, was operated by a black woman.

Because of the many boardinghouses, lunchrooms, restaurants, and taverns that sprang up across the West, white women easily found work as waitresses. But waitresses in bars and saloons had to tolerate rowdy, and sometimes lewd, behavior from customers—especially when their bosses dressed them in scanty outfits to attract business. One owner of a bar in San Francisco dressed his waitresses in ostrich-feather hats and fancy jackets, with nothing on below the waist. In Denver, the Palace Theater, which seated 750 patrons for the nightly burlesque show of bawdy skits and striptease acts and an additional 200 customers in the gambling room, featured waitresses who alternately served drinks and performed in the chorus line— which ran continuously from nine o'clock in the morning to four in the morning the next day. In Portland, Oregon, a waitress ruefully commented, "A girl has to be some sport to work in this joint." (Later, city ordinances restricted women's access to bars and saloons both as patrons and employees.)

In the 1870s, a special breed of waitress emerged— the Harvey Girl. Fred Harvey's Harvey Houses were eating establishments located at rest stops along the route of the Southwest-bound Atchison, Topeka & Santa Fe Railway, running from Chicago to California. Besides the reasonably priced and wholesome food, part of the Harvey Houses' appeal was the waitresses, who were trained to be sweet, wholesome girls with, in Fred Harvey's words, "pleasant dispositions, good manners, and an eagerness for adventure." In the January 1907 issue of *Santa Fe Magazine,* a writer captured the Harvey Girl in verse:

O the pretty Harvey Girl beside my chair,
A fairer maiden I shall never see,
She was winsome, she was neat, she was gloriously sweet,
And she was certainly good to me.

Harvey provided housing for his girls and a stern dorm mother who made sure they stayed winsome and sweet by enforcing curfews and other rules of conduct. In the early years, Harvey girls earned $17.50 a month plus room and board and tips from customers. By 1929, salaries averaged $35 a month with a $5 raise after six months. Up to 1920, the standard tip was a dime.

While many women were restricted by background or abilities to low-wage jobs as waitresses, seamstresses, domestics, and farm workers, the burgeoning cities of the West offered some women more nontraditional work. In 1889, for example, only four of the stenographers in Los Angeles were women. Four years later, there were 120 women stenographers, more than twice the number of men.

Up the coast in San Francisco, Mrs. J. W. Likins began a career as a door-to-door saleswoman, peddling engravings of President Ulysses S. Grant for a local bookseller. Despite being chased away by a shopkeeper who declared he would have "no women's rights around me," Likins was successful, and eventually expanded her territory to cover all of San Francisco and two other counties.

During a nationwide depression in 1907 teenager Frances Beebe of Pleasant Valley, Texas, found a job as an apprentice at a newspaper. She learned how to set type by hand, print and proof a galley page, and also print school catalogs and public announcements. She stayed for two years, then went to work for a newspaper in Lubbock, Texas, where she became the advertising manager. Although she earned a lower salary than her predecessor because she was a woman, she stayed on and learned every aspect of the business, from maintaining the printing presses to writing news. "It was an education and I was determined to get all of it," she said.

Even in more remote areas, women pursued innovative business ventures. On the scrappy Dakota prairie, Edith and Ida

Staff members of the Sigourney Review took to the streets of their Iowa town to promote their news-paper. Many women found work as jour-nalists, typesetters, and printers for west-ern newspapers, and some western women even established their own newspapers.

Mary Ammons stumbled into one new venture after another. First they launched a small newspaper, the *Reservation Wand*, to offer information on new farming techniques. The newspaper quickly became a voice for the region—"to acquaint the settlers with one another, to inform them of the activities going on about them, to keep them advised of frontier conditions," as Edith Ammons later explained—and a forum for tackling issues of concern to them.

They also opened a small general store to serve the settlers flocking to the area, and soon turned the store into a trading post with local Indians who brought in fence posts and berries to barter for groceries. They began to provide legal services for the Indians by publishing notices pertaining to their land affairs—"and that led, logically enough, to Ida Mary's being appointed a notary public," claimed Edith. Through publishing land claims in the *Wand*, Edith Ammons gained expertise in the complex laws governing homesteading and became a media-tor in disputes between settlers and the United States Land Office. "Slowly I was becoming identified with the land move-ment itself.... [I]n regard to conditions on the frontier [govern-ment officials] were rank amateurs and I knew it." The two sisters also conducted land transactions and received handsome commissions for their work. Other women homesteaders also combined homesteading with work such as teaching, nursing, dressmaking, cooking, or baking for hire to meet the expenses of their claims.

In 1851, Biddy Mason, an African-American slave, accompanied her master's 300-wagon train from Mississippi to California, a state that did not permit slavery. On foot, she drove his sheep the entire way. When her master tried to move his family and slaves to Texas, which upheld slavery, Mason appealed to the Los Angeles County sheriff to prevent her master from taking his slaves out of the state. In 1856, a California court granted her freedom. She worked as a nurse and midwife and saved enough to buy some land for $250. By the 1890s, a portion of the property was worth $200,000. Biddy Mason had made herself into a rich woman, and she used some of her profits to help out poor black families and to support the first African Methodist Episcopal Church in Los Angeles.

A few California women also succeeded as farmers. They brought along cows and chickens and seeds and cuttings from the East, and also learned about plants particular to the West Coast. In the 1860s, Alice Kennedy Lynch raised turkeys in San Luis Obispo County and shipped up to 700 turkeys a year to San Francisco. Sarah T. Ingall of San Jose established a dried-fruit business and shipped prunes, apricots, and peaches to the East. Down in southern California, Eliza Tibbets and her husband cultivated the first navel oranges, which became one of California's chief export crops. In nearby San Bernardino Valley, Sarah Morey opened the first nursery to sell orange trees, and down in San Diego Kate Sessions, a former teacher, planted the first gardens at Balboa Park, which later became an internationally known zoo and museum complex.

In order to work at jobs reserved for men, some women were willing to take radical steps. After her first husband died, E. J. Guerin spent 13 years impersonating a man because she thought she could make more money in a man's job. In 1850, she embarked upon a four-year stint as a boatman, working her way up from cabin boy to second waiter. At first, she was appalled by the rude and crude behavior she witnessed but gradually learned to "banish almost wholly the woman from my countenance," as she recalled later. She left the river for the rails, and in 1854 she became a brakeman on the Illinois Central Railroad. She prospected for gold in California and ran a saloon in Colorado before deciding to marry her barkeeper, H. L. Guerin—presumably after making him aware of her true identity.

There was one line of work that was even more risky and dangerous than passing as a male prospector—prostitution. As the fancy hotels and mansions went up in burgeoning western towns, so did more houses of ill repute. The first prostitutes to arrive in the gold fields came from Mexico, Peru, and Chile; they were soon followed by women from France and other European countries, as well as by Asian women and women from American cities. Native American women occasionally resorted to prostitution when they could find no other way to support themselves.

Some women came freely on their own accord to get rich, seek adventure, or find a husband. Declared one Denver prostitute: "I went into the sporting life for business reasons and no other. It was a way for a woman in those days to make money

Two prostitutes sit outside the Arizona Club. Prostitution out West was a lonely and dangerous way of life; whether they worked in fancy establishments or back-alley brothels, prostitutes were subject to disease, violence at the hands of male customers, and poverty.

and I made it." But some women were kidnapped or tricked into coming to the West. In San Francisco's Chinatown, most of the "daughters of joy" were young Chinese women who had been kidnapped, sold by their parents, or tricked into coming under the sponsorship of a "concerned" benefactor to increase their "opportunities." One young Chinese woman testified in 1892: "I was kidnapped in China and brought over here [eighteen months ago]. The man who kidnapped me sold me for four hundred dollars to a San Francisco slave-dealer; and he sold me here for seventeen hundred dollars. I have been a brothel slave ever since.... I was deceived by the promise I was going to marry a rich and good husband, or I should never have come here."

Chinese prostitution was a highly sophisticated and complex network of operations run by Chinese men who had contacts spanning the Pacific Ocean to Canton, China, and Hong Kong. When the unsuspecting women arrived on the Pacific shore, they were locked into brothel houses, forced to service a dozen or more men an evening for less than fifty cents apiece, and received no wages. Their owners made several thousand dollars a year off of each woman. Some worked in fancy parlor houses furnished in expensive teakwood and bamboo, ornamented with Chinese paintings and silk cushions, and others in tiny, sparsely furnished back-alley brothels.

Prostitution, whether by choice or coercion, was hard and dangerous. Lydia Taylor, a former prostitute who wrote an account of her life, *From Under the Lid*, to warn off other women, declared, "I could tell you stories of girls' lives that are so horrifying you would scarcely believe me." Some prostitutes committed suicide, others were killed by jealous or unhappy customers, and still others died of diseases caught from customers or became addicted to drugs or alcohol. Some prostitutes also went into debt from gambling to supplement their income. And some married as a last chance to escape from prostitution. In 1882, the Butte, Montana, *Miner* reported a "matrimonial epidemic" in the tenderloin district.

A safer and more respectable vocation for women lay in education. As in the East, teaching was the profession that employed the most women. And for black women, who mostly taught in segregated schools, and Hispanic women, who tutored or opened schools in their homes, it was the only profession that welcomed them. Ignacia Amador of California tutored soldiers' children in reading and writing in her home. Matilde Carrillo, also of California, helped teach Pío Rico, a future governor of Spanish California, to read. And Josefa Sal opened a school in San Diego, California, and taught reading, writing, and religion. But as western schools slowly expanded with the arrival of more settlers, black and Hispanic teachers unfortunately lost their jobs to whites.

Hundreds of single female teachers from the East journeyed west to teach, many of them inspired by Catharine Beecher, the visionary author of domestic manuals, who wrote: "In each neglected village, or new settlement, the Christian female teacher will quietly take her station, collecting the ignorant children around her, teaching them the habits of neatness, order and thrift; opening the book of knowledge, inspiring the principles of morality."

During the late 1840s and 1850s, Beecher raised money to establish schools in frontier communities. Some 450 teachers trained by her methods opened schools in these settlements. But "opening the book of knowledge" on the frontier was easier said than done. Teachers had to work in overcrowded, crudely built schoolrooms with pupils of widely varying abilities and few school supplies. In Ashland, Oregon, during the school year of 1859, one teacher had 28 students ranging in age from five to twenty-nine.

Rosa Kately, a single woman homesteader in McHenry County, North Dakota, taught at a schoolhouse about 15 miles from her shack. She stayed in her school during the week and rode her bicycle home every Saturday. Whenever it snowed heavily, she walked the distance because the roads were impassable by bike. She would arrive home tired, wet, and cold, build a fire to warm herself, and turn around the next day at noon to go back.

Mary Gates Haughey, who taught in the Big Gulch regions of Colorado in the 1910s, described how she and other teachers

The teachers and students of the Deadman Valley School in Colorado cheerfully pose in front of their small school. For many women in the West, teaching offered a chance to make a valuable and lasting contribution to their communities.

DEADMAN VALLEY SCHOOL DIST.NO 28 STANLEY CO.

made a home in the schoolhouse: "Some of the teachers just had a curtain back of [the schoolroom] in a corner with a stove and a bed back there, and that's the way they did at that time. There was no money for buildings to be provided for people."

Although most teachers were women, they made less than male teachers. In 1890 in Colorado, for example, women teachers earned about $6 a week, and men earned up to $8 or $9 a week. By the 1920s, female teachers in Colorado earned $75 or more a month. In San Francisco and Los Angeles, women taught primary grades, and men gravitated to better-paying high school teaching and administrative positions. By the 1880s, women made up 92 percent of public school employees and had achieved passage of a law providing equal pay for men and women teaching at the same grade level. But this legislation provided little protection for women teachers who were concentrated in the lower-paying primary grades.

Despite the low salaries and poor living and working conditions, teaching offered occupational advancement for women. Throughout the states and territories of the West, women served as principals, superintendents, and occasionally on state boards of education. In these positions, they played a vigorous and vital role in educating the children of their communities.

Many of the teachers were also missionaries, sponsored by religious organizations that had established schools on Indian reservations and in immigrant communities. In addition to teaching reading and writing, they tried to convert their students to Christianity and teach them American ways.

In San Francisco's Chinatown, missionaries made house visits to teach adult women, and started schools for Chinese children who were prohibited by law from attending public schools. From 1900 to 1914, over 200 missionary women came to Indian reservations and Hispanic settlements in New Mexico and southern Colorado alone.

Sister Blandina Segale, of the Cincinnati Sisters of Charity, was only 22 when she came to New Mexico in 1872 to establish missions and trade schools for Native Americans, but she soon became an indispensable member of the community. She prevented clashes between Indians and settlers, and galvanized entire communities to build new schoolhouses. Sister Blandina drew her bountiful energy and inspiration from the landscape itself. "Here, if you have a largeness of vision," she wrote to friends back home, "you find the opportunity to exercise it; if a cramped one, the immense expanse of the plains, the solid Rockies, the purity of the atmosphere, the faultlessness of the canopy above, will stretch the mind toward the Good.... I wish I had many hands and feet.... So much one sees to be done, and so few to do it. I have adopted this plan: Do whatever presents itself, and never omit anything because of hardship or repugnance."

Although white missionaries from the East often provided genuine assistance through their schools, many held little regard for the native cultures of their students. At mission schools on Indian reservations, Indian children were permitted to speak only English, were prohibited from wearing their native dress, and had to adopt American hairstyles. Mission teachers trained both Hispanic and Native American boys to take over traditional female agricultural tasks—tasks that had once enlarged a woman's family and village role. Alice Blake, a missionary in New Mexico, was explicit about the aims of her work: "The evolution of the Mexican home," she reported, "is now making toward Americanism."

In addition to education and religious instruction, health care had always been part of women's work in the West. Although western medical schools and state medical associations fought until the end of the 19th century to prevent women from becoming physicians, both native and settler women practiced health care in other ways. For generations, Native American and Hispanic women had served as healers and midwives, and women in newer settlements nursed their own families when no doctor was available. The Mormon communities of Utah took the lead in enabling women to get professional and medical and dental training, so that they could minister to the health needs of their people. In 1873, church leader Brigham Young urged the formation of women's classes in Salt Lake City to study physiology and obstetrics. Several Mormon women went back to the East to attend the Women's Medical College in Philadelphia. In 1882, the Woman's Relief Society, a community organization of Mormon women, founded the Deseret Hospital, a pioneer medical school headed by a female physician, which provided training in nursing and obstetrics.

Other western states followed suit. By 1893, one out of five students at medical schools in Michigan, Oregon, and Kansas were women. On the Wyoming frontier, Dr. Bessie Fell of Carpenter used a horse and buggy to make house calls over a 30-mile radius. In Nebraska, Susan La Flesche Picotte, the daughter of a chief of the Omaha tribe, pursued a remarkable career as a physician and adviser to her people. Born in 1865, she attended the Hampton Institute in Virginia, one of the few schools that admitted black and Indian students, and received her medical degree in 1889 from the Women's Medical College in Philadelphia. She graduated number one in her class and worked as an intern for one year at the Woman's Hospital in Philadelphia before returning to her people. She served first as a physician at the government school for Omaha children and eventually treated 1,300 Omahas scattered across the Omaha reservation, traveling through all kinds of weather primarily by horseback. After four years, she resigned for health reasons and opened a practice first in Bancroft, Nebraska, and then in the new town of Walthill, which was founded on the Omaha reservation.

Throughout her life, from marriage and childbirth to widowhood, raising her two sons alone, Picotte treated her fellow Omahans. She served not only as their physician but also as their health educator, scribe, translator, advocate to the U.S. government, and personal and financial adviser. Her diary recorded the many different ways that she interceded to get additional medical care for her patients, resolve disputes among them, find work for them, and help them with their financial affairs. She also helped to organize the County Medical Society of Walthill and served as chairperson of the local board of health. Her multifaceted service bridged two cultures: She acquired an education at two of the finest schools in the nation, and used her training to serve the medical and social needs of her people.

In other fields of science, women also excelled. Two women gained acclaim as nationally known botanists. Mary Katherine Curran, a physician and botanist, became curator of the Herbarium of the California Academy of Science in 1883. On her honeymoon, she and her husband walked from San Diego to San Francisco, collecting botany specimens along the way. Her successor, Alice Eastwood, stayed at the Academy for 50 years and in 1950 was elected honorary president of the Seventh International Botanical Congress in Stockholm, Sweden. Her display at the 1876 Centennial Exhibition in Philadelphia was one of the most popular booths. Martha Maxwell of Colorado gained international fame as a naturalist, taxidermist, and artist. Texan Maud Fuller Young studied biology and botany. Her book, *Mrs. Young's Familiar Lessons in Botany with Flora of Texas*, was the first science textbook written for use in Texas schools.

Women who pursued legal careers faced many of the same barriers that female physicians faced. Law schools either refused to admit them or harassed them after admission to discourage them from staying. Clara Foltz of San Jose, California, a young divorced mother with five children, worked tirelessly to achieve passage of a state law to end discrimination against women and blacks in admission to the legal profession. Several months later, Foltz, who had taught herself legal theory, was admitted to the practice of law in California. But when she tried to get formal training at the new Hastings Law School at the University of California, she was denied admission. She sued, argued her own case in court, and won. Foltz went on to practice law and achieved passage of another state law to protect women's right to pursue any lawful business or profession.

One field that did welcome women was journalism. Like Edith Ammons and Frances Beebe, women found work as reporters, typesetters, and even editors of local and regional newspapers in the West. After 1850, Ladies' Department columns began to appear in newspapers; in these columns, women writers shared recipes, sewing tips, and news and announcements about local clubs and events. Other women reporters served as outspoken advocates for women's rights.

Some women took advantage of the mining boom in the West, panning for gold right alongside their menfolk, and, if they were lucky, investing in promising mines. Mrs. E. C. Atwood of Colorado studied geology and mineralogy and worked her way up to vice president and general manager of the Bonacord Gold Mining and Milling Company. She also owned other mines throughout Colorado. Speaking from experience, she declared that mining could "be made to pay by any energetic woman who will pursue it in an intelligent way."

Anna Rich Marks, an immigrant Jewish woman from Poland (then part of Russia), made a fortune in land speculation and diamond mining. Born in poverty and haunted by the violent persecution of Jews in Russia, Marks was known to punctuate her business negotiations with a rifle in her hands. It is said that she aimed her rifle on the building of the Denver and Rio Grande railroad line until the railroad agreed to her price for crossing her land. When she died of a heart attack in 1912, she had amassed an astonishing fortune.

Like women miners and mine owners, ranchwomen often learned their craft by working right alongside their husbands, fathers, or brothers. They helped with the roundups, branded cattle, mended fences, rode the range, and retrieved strays. Bulah Rust Kirkland of Arizona found this vigorous outdoor life refreshing and told an interviewer, "I love to work with cattle and have spent a good deal of my time on the range in southern Arizona."

Some women even proved to be better ranchers than their husbands. Grace Fairchild of the Dakota Territory took over managing the family ranch after her husband nearly made them bankrupt. And Lizzie E. Johnson married a preacher who was more skilled at handling matters of the spirit than of the pocketbook. Johnson wisely kept her property and cattle in her own name and occasionally lent her husband money, always demanding repayment.

When their husbands died, widows often assumed control of the family farm or ranch. After her husband's death, Bonifacia Brady, a Hispanic farmwife in Lincoln County, New Mexico, continued to cultivate the family's 320-acre farm and care for her eight children. Her farm proved to be one of the most prosperous in Lincoln. Similarly, Ellen Casey, who also lived in Lincoln, lost her husband to the lawlessness that often plagued frontier towns. Her six children ranged in age from 18 months to 15 years. She put the older children to work planting, herding cattle, and doing other chores around the farm while she supervised the family-owned store and gristmill, and delivered flour to customers in outlying regions.

The majestic mountains, rolling hills, windswept plains and mesas, and lush forestlands of the West drew another kind of worker to the land—poets, painters, writers, and other artists who found creative inspiration in the stunning vistas and rich cultural traditions of the West. Perhaps the most well-known author of the pioneer experience was Willa Cather, who in her novels gave voice to the hopes and dreams of the last generation of homesteaders to settle the Nebraska plains. Cather, who spent her childhood years in Nebraska, worked as a journalist and

Female members of the Gabelman family at work in the strawberry patch on their Iowa farm. Some western women became accomplished farmers and cultivated new varieties of crops.

magazine writer before becoming a full-time novelist. In her fiction, she re-created a range of settings, from the Southwest and Great Plains to French Canada. But her most famous novels, *O Pioneers!* (1913) and *My Ántonia* (1918), vividly depict the life she knew so well in Nebraska. In both novels, the protagonists are strong, sturdy women settlers determined to make the land they love flourish for them.

Other women authors who wrote about the West include Laura Ingalls Wilder, who immortalized her frontier childhood in the fictionalized *Little House on the Prairie* series, and Mari Sandoz, who wrote a hauntingly poetic biography of Crazy Horse, the courageous Oglala chief who fought U.S. government troops in a daring battle that came to be known as Custer's

Last Stand, as well as other lyrical works about the American plains.

Sandoz, the daughter of German-Swiss immigrants, was born in northwestern Nebraska. Early on, she knew that she wanted to write and supported herself with various odd jobs while she wrote about her family and about Nebraska. Her many books captured not only the struggles of her immigrant parents but also the dramatic sweep of Nebraskan history. In the poetry of her prose, readers can envision the endless expanse of land and hear the wind gently whispering in the tall prairie grasses.

Less famous women also wrote about their lives in the West. Scores of Anglo women and some Indian, Hispanic, and immigrant women published memoirs about growing up or homesteading in the West. Their writings offer a vivid glimpse into the hardships and struggles, the joys and wonder of carving out a life in that rugged region—and the historical role they each played in the unfolding settlement of the West.

The splendid, sun-drenched landscape and freer way of life out West also inspired many painters and dancers. Agnes Pelton, a painter who pioneered an abstract style, lived first in Taos, New Mexico, and later near Palm Springs, California. She studied painting at the Pratt Institute in New York City and lived in Greenwich Village, a bohemian mecca in the first decades of the 20th century. But the boundless vistas and limpid light of the desert proved to be her real inspiration, and in her paintings she tried to capture the bewitching quality of the landscape in powerful abstract images. Her paintings are filled with shimmering images of rays, stars, floating orbs, and radiant lightbeams. "The vibration of this light, the spaciousness of these skies enthralled me," she wrote. "I knew there was a spirit in nature as in everything else, but here in the desert it was an especially bright spirit."

Georgia O'Keeffe, perhaps the most well-known woman painter in American history, is inextricably linked with the red cliffs and arid canyonlands of New Mexico, for these and other features of the desert landscape were her inspiration. Born in Sun Prairie, Wisconsin, she lived for a time in Texas and New

York. But when she visited New Mexico in the 1920s, she knew she had found her true home. Eventually, she resettled permanently in Abiquiu, New Mexico. Her enormous body of work captured the stark beauty and eery magic of the Southwest, and spoke with a poetry all its own. She strove, she said, to "find the feeling of infinity on the horizon line or just over the next hill." Huge red poppies and purple hollyhocks, the dry brittle canyons and mesas surrounding her home, the bleached bones of animals long perished in the broiling desert sun—these were the subjects that seized her imagination and filled her canvases.

From early childhood, Native American women learned the traditional crafts of their people, such as pottery, basketry, weaving, quilling, and painting designs on ceremonial robes. But throughout the late 19th century and into the 20th, several Indian women emerged as talented portrait painters as well. Among them was Narcissa Chisholm Owen, a Cherokee born in Oklahoma Territory, who fought against racial and sexual prejudice through her art. She challenged popular images of Indians as primitive, scalp-wielding savages, and instead depicted the strength and dignity of her people.

"The facts are," she declared, "the Indians of Indian Territory are civilized, educated Christian people.… [M]y painting

The beauty of the western landscape offered artistic inspiration to countless women. Here, members of a local art club paint on a California beach around 1890.

was not done in a tepee, but on Pennsylvania Avenue...in Washington, D.C." Owen enjoyed a life of privilege. She was the daughter of an Irish mother and a Native American father who was the last hereditary chief of part of the Cherokee nation. Owen grew up in an affluent household with slaves, attended schools run by missionaries, and married a wealthy business-man. In her art, Owen strove to unite the two worlds in which she had lived—Native American and Anglo—and celebrate the unique dignity of an individual who embraced both cultures.

Thousands of other Indian women artists created pottery, weaving, beadwork, and basketry. Practicing these traditional arts and crafts helped to preserve and transmit their cultural traditions—especially after the massive influx of settlers had begun to alter both the landscape and patterns of life in Indian communities—and to earn a living in an economy that was changing from one based on trade to one based on cash. Artwork allowed Indian women to earn money while remaining at home rather than working in poorly paid jobs, usually as domestics, for Anglo settlers. By the late 19th century, native women's arts and crafts had become collectors' items and were bought by settlers, tourists, and dealers who found a growing market for these crafts back East.

The rich, diverse landscape and history of the West inspired many other female artists from a variety of backgrounds. As Mormon Utah painter Minerva Kohlhepp Teichert declared, "Unless I can paint a little each day on the great pageant of the West I think the day is lost. It seems like a call to me that I sin if I while my time away and do not answer."

Two of the dance world's most daring and original spir-its—Isadora Duncan and Martha Graham—grew up in California and, like Teichert, found their inspiration in the pageantry of the West. Duncan, who was born in San Francisco, enjoyed a free and unfettered childhood. Her mother introduced her to the creative magic of poetry, dance, music, and nature. After studying classical ballet, Duncan rejected the rigid, intri-cate movements of this dance form and sought instead to recapture the flowing, expressive movements that had shaped ancient dancing. She studied sculpture and drew inspiration from the hauntingly dramatic landscape of the Bay Area to express the spectrum of human emotions, from joy to despair. As she later wrote in her memoirs, "My life and my art were born of the sea.... I was already a dancer and a revolutionist." American audiences shunned her daring new style of dancing; they were shocked by her filmy, revealing costumes and her desire to showcase the human body in motion. Duncan found a much more responsive audience in Europe, and after 1900 she lived primarily in western Europe and Russia. Despite her inability to reach American audiences, she was a true pioneer— not only in the new, more flowing and expressive dance form she created but in her passion to celebrate the joy and mystery of human existence, in dance as well as in her life.

Martha Graham was born in Pennsylvania but spent her teenage years in southern California, where she first discovered the art form of dance. Like Duncan, she was a maverick who rewrote the rules. She introduced a provocative new style of dance, at once more spontaneous and expressive than the rigid, formal style of classical ballet. In her dancing and her choreography—the process of creating dance steps to a piece of music—Graham aspired, in her words, to "chart the graph of the heart"—to portray through movement the mysteries of the human psyche. For her, dancing was a deeply personal "affirmation of life."

Graham explored many provocative ideas through her dances. In the 1930s, during the worst economic depression the country has ever known, she choreographed dances that celebrated the American spirit and American traditions. *Two Primitive Canticles, Primitive Mysteries*, and *Ceremonials* explored the cultural traditions and rituals of Native Americans. *Appalachian Spring* was a tribute to the strength and spirit of the pioneers, and *Letter to the World* portrayed the life and poetry of American poet Emily Dickinson. Like Duncan, Graham was a pioneer who demonstrated the dazzling power of dance to communicate the mysteries of human existence.

Two cowgirls ride into the ring at the start of a Wild West show in Oklahoma. Being cowgirls offered women a life of adventure and freedom from many of the restraints governing women's lives.

Physicians and lawyers, seamstresses and saloon keepers, boardinghouse matrons and madams, bakers, cooks, cowhands, teachers, journalists, and artists—western women took full advantage of the opportunities available to them, and they challenged barriers on all fronts. William Brewer, a pioneer in California in the 1860s, recalled an encounter that symbolized the new freedom among western women. As he was bent over his washtub, two women "who were assisting as vaqueros [cowboys]" rode up on their horses. A rodeo was in progress nearby, and these women, the wife and daughter of a rancher, had come to help rope cattle. "Well mounted, they managed their horses superbly, and just as I was up to my elbows in soapsuds, along they came, with a herd of several hundred cattle.... I straightened my aching back, drew a long breath and must have blushed...and reflected on the doctrine of woman's rights—I, a stout man, washing my shirt, and those ladies practicing the art of vaqueros."

CHAPTER 7

"THERE WAS A SPIRIT OF HELPFULNESS"

BUILDING NEW COMMUNITIES

Almost as soon as they settled into their new homes and planted their crops or staked their claims, women and men set about completing another task—creating the schools, churches, organizations, and other signposts of community life.

Their first efforts to build new communities centered around simple, good-neighborly mutual assistance, such as quilting and cheese-making parties and helping each other bring in the harvest. Alice Lund, whose family and another family immigrated from Sweden to Minnesota and then to Wisconsin, described why the two families settled adjoining claims and built their log cabins close to each other—"to make it convenient for water, mutual aid and the joy and comfort of close fellowship."

In the early stages of building a community, neighbors helped each other. Lorencita Miranda, a Hispanic resident of Lincoln County, New Mexico, recalled that in her early years there "[people] helped each other with their work. If someone was building a home, neighbors would help build it. If wheat was being cut, everyone would gather to help....Women friends would help their neighbor when they had a bunch of men to

Residents of a Kansas town stand outside their church. The construction of churches, schools, and other public buildings were visible signs of homesteaders' eagerness to establish permanent communities.

feed." Neighbors helping each other, and neighbors working together to build a community—this quest for fellowship coexisted with the quest for personal prosperity. Settlers went west for better economic opportunities and for adventure, but as more families homesteaded they also wanted to create a morally upright social order. Schools and churches began to appear when more families settled a particular area. In a Washington, Colorado, settlement composed mostly of Danish bachelors, no school was built for more than ten years until families with children arrived.

Women often took the lead in organizing schools and churches. They did not want their children to grow up without an education. In 1878, Anne LeGrand of Texas wrote to her mother, "It makes me feal sorry to See them growing up in ignorance. Mollie can Spell & read a little but Julie dount no her letters. I am going to get them some books and try to learn them at home." Married women often set up the first schools in their homes. But these schools usually met for only a few months a year.

The West was the only part of the nation in which over half of all African-American girls of high school age attended school. Black families were eager to send their daughters to school while their sons stayed home and worked, because they knew that education was the key to advancement for black women.

Women's sense of their family duties not only inspired them to make a home in the wilderness but to get involved in their communities to help improve the quality of life for their families. They sponsored box lunches and bazaars, dances and theatricals, and other events to raise funds for the schools and churches that would educate their children and protect their families' piety.

In one Oklahoma community, the Ladies Aid Society raised the money to pay the teacher. Elsewhere, women even helped to build the schoolhouse. Mabel Sharpe Beavers claimed that her local school board "took up collections and bought rough lumber, and they and the pupils and I built that school house with our own hands." In Oregon in the 1850s, Tabitha Brown, a widow and grandmother, donated land, a house, $550 of her earnings, and a bell for a schoolhouse. She also fought to keep the school open.

Civilizing the West not only meant building schools and churches, but combating vice and immorality and establishing wholesome community activities. Women spearheaded campaigns to abolish prostitution and the consumption of alcohol, and organized reading clubs, debating societies, amateur musical and dramatic groups, and libraries. Effie Vivian Smith of Burke County, North Dakota, wrote to her cousin about the debate that her newly formed literary society held: "The question was Resolved that city life is better than country life. All the judges decided in the negative. I was on and was so scared I didn't know what to do. Next Fri. I am on again & the question is: Is marriage a failure?" Some of these events and activities were open to women only, but some welcomed the entire family. Dances, picnics, box suppers, spelling bees, baseball games, card parties, debates, and dramatic readings drew men as well as women, and young and old alike.

After the Civil War, a remarkable movement swept the nation—women across the country organized clubs to develop common interests and work together to improve their communities. Some were study clubs devoted to learning; others were organizations designed to raise money for building schools, hospitals, orphanages, and other public facilities; and others were religious groups. But many were intent on improving social and economic conditions for women, children, and ethnic minorities.

Western women eagerly joined this movement, and they organized clubs in their new communities with astonishing speed. Within a year of settlement, Wichita and Dodge City, both in Kansas, boasted an array of women's organizations. In Galesburg, Illinois, women immediately formed a Moral Reform Society, as well as two prayer meetings, a mothers' association, and a sewing society. These and other clubs played a vital role in improving new communities.

Even clubs that were devoted to socializing or to self-study benefited the larger community. Aggie Loring of Arizona proudly wrote her mother in 1876, "We have a Literary Association. We are to use the funds for a Public Library. They have decided to have the library in our store and have chosen me for Librarian." In Houston, Texas, the Ladies Reading Club shared rooms with the Houston Library and later helped to pay the library's moving expenses to a new building. And throughout Texas, women's clubs lobbied for better schools and more funding for public education, raised money for scholarships and loan funds for women, and worked for laws regulating child labor. In 1911 in Texas, the Federation of Women's Clubs and the Congress of Mothers lobbied successfully for a law prohibiting children under 15 from working in factories and mills, and banning children under 17 from jobs in mining, quarrying, and other dangerous occupations.

In Florence, Arizona, women spearheaded efforts to clean up the town's dirty streets, erect street signs, and incorporate the town. In 1870, Rosa Newmark of Los Angeles organized the Ladies' Hebrew Benevolent Society to care for ailing and dying women within the town's small Jewish community. Up north Jewish women in San Francisco established a settlement house for east European immigrants. The facility offered vocational training and education in American culture, a kindergarten, gymnasium, medical clinic, and a residence for single Jewish women.

Also in San Francisco, Chinese women formed the Chinese Women's Jeleab (self-reliance) Association. Patterned after a Chinese men's benevolent group, which barred women from joining, the organization drew on American ideals of individual freedom and equality, as well as the Chinese cultural tradition of mutual cooperation. Liu Yilan, a club member, said, "Our goal is to cultivate self-reliance in each of us and, further, to promote and propagate this concept in China, so as to strip away the black curtain that has blocked our [women's] view of the sky for thousands of years."

In 1887, in Helena, Montana, women formed the Poor Relief Committee. They determined who among the town's poor was eligible for relief, arranged for donations of goods from local merchants, distributed the money allocated by the town to the poor, and maintained financial records.

For Hilda Rose of Montana, membership in the local Helping Hand club inspired her to reach out to women she once would have scorned as crude or immoral. Her club included members who had borne children out of wedlock, had carried on love affairs with married men who were not their husbands, and were "used to fighting and hair pulling." Rose's husband urged her not to socialize with such coarse women for fear the "nice women on the prairie" would rebuff her. But she did not listen to him. "Maybe Daddy [her husband] is right," she wrote. "I'll confess this much. I don't feel the aversion I used to to a fallen woman.... One day a girl of sixteen came to a school entertainment in our schoolhouse here and she had in her arms a six-weeks-old illegitimate child by a married man. She was there on a seat all alone, and I just picked myself up and went and sat down beside her and held the baby for her."

But not every clubwoman was so accepting. When the women of Newcastle, Wyoming, organized a women's club and put a notice in the local newspaper inviting "any and every woman" to attend the first meeting, the town's prostitutes and

Women's clubs that aimed to help the community sprang up throughout the West and provided club members with important leadership skills.

dancehall girls came. To discourage these women of the night from joining, the club developed a policy requiring homework, which these women had no time to do.

Western women accomplished a good deal in their clubs but not without overcoming obstacles. The long distances between homesteads and poor roads, especially during winter, thwarted women's attempts to meet regularly. In many western communities, settlers were constantly moving out for better opportunities elsewhere, making it nearly impossible to establish stable club membership and programs. Wrote one frustrated young woman who had tried to organize a club: "Everyday parties are leaving.... I often ask myself what shall be my course of conduct, how shall I live in such a community.... Shall I too selfishly address myself to money getting and ignore the claims of society upon me, or shall my influence be used to bring about a better state of things and beget a little public spirit."

Black settlers had to form their own communities and organizations, for the social and economic opportunities that the West offered did not mean an end to discrimination. Many black women's clubs grew out of their churchwork or started out as mutual-benefit or literary societies that gradually evolved into community service groups. In Kansas, during the 1880s, African-American women embarked on an ambitious club movement. The first clubs were devoted to literary study, needlework, and charity. Like black clubwomen elsewhere, Kansas clubwomen strove to create organizations that promoted the dignity and virtues of black womanhood and that served their families' and communities' needs. By the early 20th century, Kansas clubwomen had joined the National Association of Colored Women, a national federation of black women's clubs, and had also formed their own state federation. As the years progressed, they shifted their focus from self-education and self-improvement to creating scholarships for black youth and sponsoring more charity projects.

By the 1920s, between 500 and 700 black women belonged to clubs in Kansas, and in 1924 Kansas's black clubwomen spearheaded a new project—to organize young black girls and

The members of Salt Lake City's First Ward Relief Society. Mormon women formed their own clubs to aid the needy in their community.

women into junior clubs. That year, the first junior club in Kansas was organized. In 1925, junior club members called for the Kansas public schools to use books and pamphlets providing "fair and impartial treatment of the position and accomplishments of the American Negro in History, Art, Science, and War." Black clubwomen and girls in Kansas worked together, sharing ideas and skills, affirming the worth and dignity of black womanhood, and helping themselves and their race.

Elsewhere in the West, black women eagerly formed clubs. The Woman's Day Nursery Association of Los Angeles, formed in 1908, and other African-American mothers' clubs provided child care for black mothers who worked, and also endeavored to raise wages and improve working conditions for black women. Another Los Angeles club, the Sojourner Truth Industrial Club, provided a shelter for orphans and unwed mothers along with training in domestic service, and strove, according to its charter, to instill "intellectual and moral culture." The club's building, completed in 1913, served as a home as well as a community center; upper-class black women sponsored teas, lectures, and lessons in needlecraft for the home's residents. In 1906, black women's clubs in California joined together to form a State Federation of Colored Women's Clubs, and by 1920 black clubwomen in other western states had formed similar federations.

Mormon women also formed their own groups. Throughout the 19th century they organized Relief Societies to carry out a variety of community tasks, such as making clothing and linens for Native American women; arranging for domestic services for the sick, disabled, widowed, and orphaned; delivering babies; and providing clothing for the dead and meals for the grieving. Through their Relief Societies, they also managed their settlements' general stores, dairies, woolen mills, and telegraph networks; stimulated new home-industry programs for making silk, weaving textiles, and sewing clothes; and helped educate the settlement's children. The many domestic and social and economic activities of Mormon women enabled their settlements to thrive and remain self-sufficient—that is, able to survive the social and economic rejection of the non-Mormon world.

Looking beyond their own communities' needs, western women joined a variety of political and social movements to expand their political rights and bring about economic justice. Throughout the Midwest and far West, women joined the Grange movement, an organization of farmers that was established in 1867 to improve agricultural conditions and promote their economic interests. The first branches, called Granges, were located in Minnesota. Members established cooperative organizations to buy seeds and supplies at low cost and to sell their crops. Female Grange members experimented with cooperative kitchens and advocated more comfortable clothing for women, greater control over their own property, and the right to vote.

Loosely associated with the Grange movement was the Farmers' Alliance and its successor, the Populist party, which was established in 1890. Both the Alliance and the Populist party recruited women as lecturers and organizers and supported women's right to vote, and here, too, women were energetically involved. Mary E. Lease of Kansas and Luna Kellie of

Nebraska both served as speakers and recruiters for their state chapters of the Farmers' Alliance and the Populist party. The Alliance developed programs to benefit farmers, including educational programs; associations for cooperative buying, marketing, and warehousing; and other strategies to improve farmers' economic status.

Its successor, the Populist party, converted these individual programs into a wide-ranging political platform designed to protect farmers' interests in an economy that catered increasingly to industrial and financial interests—"a government of Wall Street, by Wall Street, and for Wall Street," as Mary E. Lease bitingly declared. Lease gained a reputation as a quick-tongued speaker. Wrote one western farmer in his diary: "Went to town to hear Joint discussion between Mrs. Lease and John M. Brumbaugh. Poor Brumbaugh was not in it." In 1891, Lease helped to establish the National Woman's Alliance, a separate Populist women's organization devoted to carrying out the precepts of Populism and promoting complete social and political equality between the sexes.

In mining camps and towns, women fought alongside men to force mine owners to improve living and working conditions. Mining was especially dangerous work. Accidents and explosions in underground mines maimed or killed thousands of miners each year. Miners in Colorado lived in primitive conditions in towns that were mostly controlled by giant mining interests. Miners lived in houses built by their employers, bought their food and household necessities at company-owned stores, and sent their children to company-run schools. Their lives were subject to the whims and self-interest of their employers, wealthy and powerful mining magnates.

To make matters worse, a miner's life was peripatetic—he moved himself and his family from one camp to another,

The Grange movement began in Minnesota in 1867 as an attempt by farmers to improve agricultural conditions and advance their economic interests. Branches quickly spread throughout the West, including this one in Texas.

wherever he could find work. But miners learned to fight together for better salaries and working conditions. Throughout Colorado, during the first two decades of the 20th century, striking miners and the militia dispatched by mine owners to quell them clashed in several violent incidents. In 1914, militia in Ludlow, Colorado, on hand to stop 9,000 striking miners, opened machine gun fire on the miners and their families. Not only miners but many women and children were brutally killed in what came to be known as the Ludlow Massacre. This massacre led to ten days of rebellion throughout Colorado.

During strikes, women and children in mining towns yelled at the militia, threw stones, distributed strike relief, and helped protect their homes. May Wing, of Cripple Creek, Colorado, recalled that her aunt, Hannah Welch, kept two "great big butcher knives…razor sharp," and "she always said if one of those militia men ever come in her house in the middle of the night, they'd leave with less than they brought in!"

Other women learned the power of collective action. In Seattle, San Francisco, and Los Angeles, waitresses formed their own labor unions to fight for higher wages and improved working conditions. In Butte, Montana, black and white women janitors, dishwashers, cooks, and waitresses organized a union that in 1907 forced employers to reduce the workday from 14 hours to 8.

In 1890, seamstresses organized the Cooperative Shirtmakers of the Pacific Coast. Female laundry workers in California formed the Steam Laundry Workers Union. Boot and shoe workers struck over working conditions in 1891. Glove workers in Northern California struck to protest having to pay for electricity and rental fees for their sewing machines. These are just some of the labor actions that western workers undertook to improve their work lives.

Besides organizing clubs and collective activities, women also sought political power to have a greater voice in the communities they were building. Like women in the East, western women sought the right to vote in all elections, especially Presidential elections. The organized American women's rights movement began in 1848 when Elizabeth Cady Stanton,

Lucretia Mott, and three other women's rights advocates organized a convention in the tiny hamlet of Seneca Falls, New York. For two days, about 300 participants, including 40 men, debated and voted in favor of several resolutions demanding women's right to vote, to maintain ownership of their property after marriage, to sign contracts and keep custody of their children after divorce, and to enter professions closed to them, such as law and medicine. They framed their demands in their manifesto, "The Declaration of Sentiments and Resolutions." This document charted the goals and activities of the American women's rights movement for many decades to come.

Though all American women did not gain the right to vote until 1920, when the 19th Amendment to the U.S. Constitution was finally ratified, some women in the West were voting as early as 1869. That year, the Wyoming Territorial Legislature passed a law granting all women in Wyoming, regardless of color or economic status, the right to vote. The bill also permitted Wyoming women to hold office and serve on juries. In February 1870, Esther Morris was appointed to serve as Justice of the Peace, the first woman justice on record. Twenty years later, Wyoming entered the union as the first state to grant women the right to vote.

The Utah territorial legislature followed Wyoming's example and granted women the vote in 1870. Proponents and critics of polygamy supported the suffrage bill for very different reasons: Mormon male leaders hoped that Mormon women would vote to preserve their practice of polygamy, and critics hoped that women would vote to abolish polygamy.

Utah's Mormon women eagerly supported woman suffrage. But from 1886 to 1895, all of Utah's women and polygamy-practicing men lost the right to vote when the U.S. Congress passed legislation to outlaw plural marriages. Finally, in 1896, the Mormon Church renounced polygamy and Utah was admitted to the union. With statehood, Utah's women regained the right to vote.

By 1912, the only nine states that granted women the right to vote were in the West and Midwest: Wyoming (which

Nevada governor Emmett D. Boyle signs a resolution calling for the Nevada Assembly to ratify the 19th Amendment to the Constitution, which would grant women the right to vote. Some of the earliest victories in the battle for woman suffrage were won in western states and territories.

Gov. Emmett D. Boyle of Nevada signing resolution for ratification of Nineteenth Amendment to Constitution of U.S. - Mrs. Sadie D. Hurst who presented the resolution Speaker of the Assembly J.J. Fitzgerald and group of Suffrage Women - Feb-7-1920
CARSON CITY - NEVADA

gave women the right to vote in 1869), Utah (1870), Colorado (1893), Idaho (1896), Washington (1910), California (1911), and Oregon, Kansas, and Arizona (1912). Alaska granted female suffrage in 1913, and Montana and Nevada followed in 1914. Among the western states, only New Mexico did not grant women the right to vote until the 19th Amendment to the Constitution was ratified in 1920.

What accounted for the victories out West? Perhaps because these states were recently settled and had no deeply established tradition of social and political inequality, territorial legislators were more willing to grant woman suffrage. Suffrage leaders also argued that women needed the ballot to protect themselves from the unruly aspects of western life. In 1872, suffragist Nettie C. Tator made this argument before a legislative committee in California: "There is more individuality of character here for both sexes, and fewer social restraints, therefore a greater tendency toward license, which makes it all the more necessary for [woman] to have it in her power to protect herself through making the laws of the land."

In the region that is now Oregon and Washington, Abigail Scott Duniway led the fight for woman suffrage. At 17, she journeyed in 1852 with her family by wagon train to the Oregon Territory. There she married and raised five children and discovered firsthand what toiling long hours for no wages meant: "To sew and cook, and wash and iron; to bake and clean and stew and fry; to be, in short, a general pioneer drudge, with never a penny of my own, was not pleasant business for an erstwhile school teacher," she wrote later. She also discovered that even though wives had no legal rights, a wife was responsible for any financial obligations undertaken by her husband. When Duniway's husband became incapacitated, she was forced to pay off his debts.

By the age of 36, Duniway had established her own newspaper, the *New Northwest*, to campaign for suffrage. She also crisscrossed the region to give speeches and help organize suffrage events. Duniway clashed with suffrage leaders in the East over strategy, but her ideas prevailed out West. She was brisk and hardy, and fiercely devoted to seeking more social and political power for women.

Among the most outspoken of women reformers were newspaper reporters and editors like Duniway. In her Denver-based newspaper, the *Queen Bee*, Caroline N. Churchill, a women's rights advocate, carried news about conventions and other events pertaining to the women's rights movement. She faithfully reprinted the speeches of major suffragists such as Elizabeth Cady Stanton and Susan B. Anthony, and urged her readers to support the cause.

Sara Isadore Sutherland, who wrote under the pen name Pauline Periwinkle, launched a weekly women's page in the *Dallas Morning News* to spearhead much-needed social reforms in Texas. Under the heading "The Woman's Century," Periwinkle urged her readers to organize a public library and to expand women's educational opportunities, from free kindergartens to more colleges. She also called for the creation of juvenile courts and detention homes to address the special needs of young offenders, the construction of more playgrounds in and around Dallas, a law to ensure sanitary food preparation, and laws prohibiting wage discrimination against women. Some of her

Caroline N. Churchill used her Denver-based newspaper, the Queen Bee, *to promote the women's rights movement.*

ideas came to fruition; inspired by her column, the Dallas Federation of Women's Clubs organized a public library as its first project.

In her columns, Periwinkle pointed out the social needs and problems in Dallas and described how other communities around the nation tackled similar problems. She was an ardent clubwoman and helped to organize the Dallas Federation of Women's Clubs, the Equal Suffrage Club of Dallas, the Dallas Women's Forum, and the Texas Woman's Press Association. She urged clubwomen to shift their focus from "eatables and wearables" to "thinkables and doables," and inspired many of the social and political reforms that Dallas's clubwomen achieved. Like other western newspaperwomen, she used her newspaper, and her vision, to promote better living conditions in the young and growing communities of the West.

Women who were part of ethnic minorities in the West could not confine their activism to labor concerns or the suffrage movement. They also had to battle for basic freedoms that white women already enjoyed. In San Francisco, Sieh King King, an 18-year-old student and an immigrant from Tianjin, China, boldly condemned foot-binding, a centuries-old Chinese tradition in which young girls' feet were tightly bound to keep them from growing—and to keep women from freely moving around. Sieh King King declared that men and women were equals and deserved the same rights and privileges, including education and a voice in public affairs.

Another organization that worked to improve Chinese women's lives was the YWCA (Young Women's Christian Association), which opened a branch in San Francisco's Chinatown in 1916. Though a white woman headed the facility, the board of directors was composed primarily of Chinese women. From the start, the Chinatown YWCA offered English classes, advice on household hygiene and baby care, and social activities. During the 1920s, the YWCA helped to investigate and improve working conditions at factories that employed Chinese women.

Between 1875 and 1916, Margaret Culbertson and later Donaldina Cameron and other volunteer women of the Presbyterian Women's Home Society rescued Chinese and Japanese girls who had been forced into prostitution by unscrupulous agents posing as the girls' protectors. They carefully planned their rescues and encountered little opposition from Chinese guards who often turned and fled at the sight of these women striding briskly toward them. The society managed to rescue 30 to 40 prostitutes a year and housed them in a mission. But the society imposed a different kind of regimen on the former prostitutes by pressuring them to conform to American cultural values and to enter marriages that were not always happy or compatible, and these unfortunate young Chinese women still had little control over their lives.

Finally, in 1880, western legislatures began to pass laws to control prostitution. And in the early 1900s, moral reformers shut down the most blatant parlor houses, and prostitution went underground.

Like the Pueblo Indian women of New Mexico who built and plastered the adobe structures in their villages, later generations of western women built the foundations and structures for new communities out West. But into their communities they also built boundaries and walls between residents of different ethnic backgrounds. Discrimination against African Americans, Asian Americans, Hispanics, and people of different religious orientations remained as strong and sturdy as the new buildings going up in every western community.

On stagecoaches in Kansas and Colorado and streetcars in San Francisco, black women were barred from using public transportation. Restaurants outside of the black community often refused to serve blacks, and theaters and department stores barred them from entering. Nor could they rent rooms in

The members of the Iowa Association of Colored Women's Clubs gather for a group portrait. Black women countered the discrimination and isolation they faced in western communities by forming their own clubs and organizations.

most hotels or use public recreation facilities. Ruth Flowers, who was 15 when she moved to Colorado with her family in 1917, recalled: "You couldn't go in any restaurant, any hot dog stand, any ice cream parlor, any movies—you could go no place, absolutely no place." Until 1880, many western states prevented blacks from attending white public schools and failed to provide school facilities for black students. It was left to frontier black communities to find quarters for their schools.

Because of such searing discrimination, and because blacks were scattered far and wide, they felt even more isolated out West. Emma Ray, a black missionary in Seattle, remembered, "There were but few of our own people in Seattle when we came in 1889 and at times I got very lonely."

For more than 40 years, starting in 1912, Charlotte Spears Bass, an African-American woman, edited the Los Angeles–based *California Eagle*, an early black newspaper on the West Coast. In its pages, she decried racism and discrimination against blacks. In 1952, she became the first black woman to run for the Vice Presidency of the United States.

Other black women sued in court to obtain social and legal rights. In Riverside, California, a black woman instituted the first lawsuit in California against barring blacks from public swimming pools. Sadie Cole, also of California, launched a campaign to remove "Negroes not wanted" signs from eating establishments after being overcharged for a glass of buttermilk.

Some African-American women joined women of other races in the voting rights movement. They campaigned for suffrage to combat racial discrimination as well as sexual inequality. Although the 15th Amendment to the Constitution, ratified in 1870, prohibited the denial of voting rights to black men because of their race, local and state governments throughout the country, including the West, found ways to deny black men of their lawful right to vote. Naomi Anderson of Kansas, an official representative of the National American Woman Suffrage Association, the central women's rights organization, helped to lead campaigns in Kansas and California. And Sarah M. Overton led suffrage groups in San Jose, California, and traveled throughout the state in 1911 to marshal blacks' support for the state's female suffrage amendment.

Others sought to create communities where blacks could live in dignity and prosperity, free from the bonds of racial discrimination. In 1910, in Dearfield, Colorado, about 70 miles from Denver, Oliver T. Jackson established an all-black farming community. He hoped to provide vocational and agricultural training on the land so that blacks could become self-sufficient farmers and merchants. He purchased land, and gradually his tiny pioneer settlement grew into a prosperous farming community of about 700 people. Dearfield—so named, as one black homesteader explained, because the "land was dear to us"— flourished for two decades until a drought destroyed its farms. Said Eunice Norris, another resident, "People got along well. It was a peaceful sort of situation: struggling people working hard; they didn't have time for trouble. There was a spirit of helpfulness." Another former resident recalled, "I remember places in Dearfield where they had dances, a dancehall. There were moonlight picnics, with lanterns, and big chicken fries. The people were friendly, neighborly."

Separate, all-black communities, like Dearfield, offered an oasis of hope and opportunity for black homesteaders who had encountered bigotry and scarce economic opportunities in other western settlements. Wherever they could, black migrants formed their own communities to pursue shared goals and a close-knit social and religious life. But, like Dearfield, most of these communities failed for lack of money, and their inhabitants were forced to return to mostly white settlements, where they faced social and economic discrimination.

Relations between settlers and the original inhabitants of the land—Native Americans—continued to be marred by ignorance, intolerance, and mutual suspicion. After the Civil War, as more settlers headed west, the U.S. government pursued a ruthless policy of forcing Native Americans to resettle on reservations. These designated patches of land, which served as their homes and farmlands, were wholly inadequate to support the masses of native peoples herded onto them. On the reservations, government officials pressured Indian men to take over farming tasks, excluding Indian women from agricultural activities that once gave meaning and importance to their lives. Indian women still planted private vegetable gardens and gathered wild foods, but they lost status and independence as the men began to control family land and income. The U.S. government also tried to turn Indians into homesteaders. The Dawes Act of 1887, which governed Indian relations until 1934, further eroded traditional gender roles and kinship relations by assigning homesteads to nuclear Indian families, consisting only of two parents and their children. The act granted 160 acres to

A map of the all-black town of Dearfield, Colorado. Such settlements were a way for blacks to escape the bigotry and lack of economic opportunities they encountered throughout the West.

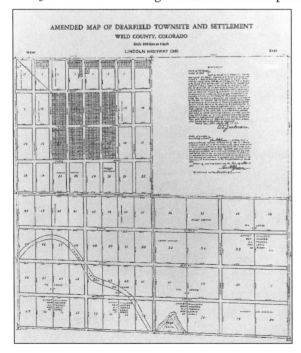

a family and 80 acres to an individual, following a 25-year period in which the land was held in federal trust. The act aspired to speed the assimilation of Indians into mainstream America—but, in reality, it further undermined tribal cultures and reduced the total amount of land owned by Indians, resulting in further deprivation and suffering.

Indian families not only lost control over their land, they also lost control over their children and native customs. Prior to World War I, Navajo families in New Mexico were required by the U.S. government to send at least one child to boarding schools where he or she would learn Anglo ways. This policy was yet another part of a national plan to replace the traditional skills of Indian men and women with the skills of Anglo culture. In many of these schools, Indian children were forbidden to speak their native languages. Lucy Swan, a Sioux woman born on the Rosebud Reservation in South Dakota in 1900, recalled how she learned to speak English and read the Bible in a government-sponsored school. "They [the teachers] don't let us talk Indian among each other. You have to talk English all the time. And they so strict....We have to wear high-topped shoes and black stockings and long dresses."

Settlers and other outsiders regarded Indian dances and ceremonies with a mixture of curiosity and disdain, and sometimes even revulsion. During the 1870s and 1890s, western Indian tribes engaged in religious revivals that relied heavily on dances. These "Ghost Dances," as they were called, were performed to preserve native cultural traditions and to counteract the power and presence of Anglos. In the 1870s, many of these dances openly expressed hostile sentiments against Anglos. In response, the U.S. government forbade such dances.

Between 1873 and 1912, the Mescalero Apache of New Mexico were prohibited from performing dances that celebrated young women's coming of age. The federal government condemned these and similar dances as subversive. Government officials also regulated where other Indian dances could be performed, and allowed public performances only at Wild West shows, fairs, and at the Indian pueblos of New Mexico.

Indian men and women bravely stood up to whites' abuses of their land and people. Like whites, they viewed people different from themselves with a mixture of suspicion and disdain. Annie Lowry, half Piute, declared, "We have learned, as a race, very little from the white people that has been helpful. Sometimes I wonder at the white people who are so smart and think they know so much. They do things as dumb as Indians in spite of all their high falutin' talk." Maria Chona, a Papago Indian, turned her nose up at the food that whites ate: "I think it has no strength. My grandchildren make me gruel out of wild seeds. That is food."

Indian women despaired at how whites destroyed their land. Pretty Shield, a Crow woman, vividly described the ruination that whites had brought upon her land: "The tree says, 'Don't. I am sore. Don't hurt me.' But they chop it down and cut it up. The spirit of the land hates them.... The Indian never hurts any thing, but the white people destroy all.... How can the spirit of the earth like the white man? That is why God will upset the world—because it is sore all over. Everywhere the white man has touched it, it is sore." Indian physician Susan La Flesche Picotte likened the whites to a "huge plough" which had buried "into the darkness of the earth every hope and aspiration which we have cherished."

In the 1880s, Sarah Winnemucca, the daughter of a Piute chief from Nevada, emerged as a forceful spokeswoman for her people. After witnessing a forced march of Piutes from Nevada to Washington Territory during the bitter winter of 1878, she testified before President Rutherford B. Hayes and Secretary of the Interior Carl Schurz. In 1881, she went on a lecture tour to publicize the hardships of that forced march and other wrongs committed against the Piutes, and later published her lectures in a book, *Life Among the Piutes*. Although she was unsuccessful in securing better treatment for her people, she had shown remarkable courage and determination in publicly voicing her outrage. Her forceful words aroused public sympathy, if not action, on behalf of her people.

Like Sarah Winnemucca, Helen Hunt Jackson, a native New Englander, made it her life's work to expose injustices against Native Americans. She moved to Colorado to research the problems, and in 1881 published *A Century of Dishonor*, a scathing indictment of governmental policy toward Indian tribes. At her own expense, she sent copies of her book, bound in blood-red covers, to government officials, including every member of Congress.

Three years later, she published *Ramona*, a historical novel about a Native American woman in California. "I did not write *Ramona*," she later declared. "It was written through me. My life-blood went into it—all I had thought, felt and suffered for five years on the Indian question." Though simplistic and sentimental, the novel focused public attention on the plight of Native Americans and earned Jackson an enduring reputation as a western novelist.

In rare cases, settlers over-came racial barriers to build strong friendships. Era Bell Thompson and her parents and two brothers, black settlers on the North Dakota prairie, happily discovered that their nearest neighbor, Carl Brendel, a German immigrant, did not let bigotry interfere with generosity. When Brendel—or "Big Carl," as he was more commonly known—learned that Era Bell and her family had only boiled potatoes to eat, he brought them a 100-pound sack of flour, a big sack of sugar, canned goods, meat, lard—and candy for little Era Bell. Her father explained to Brendel that he couldn't pay him for his

Sarah Winnemucca became a powerful spokeswoman for Native American rights.

kindness because he had no money. Brendel scoffed and said, "I no vant money.... I your neighbor, I help you. Dot iss all." The Thompsons, in turn, helped Brendel and their other neighbor, Gus, also from Europe, harvest their grain.

Occasionally, friendships blossomed between women of diverse backgrounds. Alice Lund recalled how Indian women visited her family's cabin, "bringing their papooses along. Mother very often made coffee for them. They could not talk to each other. They always seemed to enjoy the visit. Mother and our neighbor lady always returned their calls and of course we children always went along. We would go from one wigwam to the other, but we favored two families, so we spent more time at their places. Mother showed interest in their handwork and also the way they did their cooking."

Korean immigrant Mary Paik recalled how the mothers of her Hispanic classmates got together on rainy days and made tamales for all of the students. "The Mexican families were so generous—they always remembered to make extra ones for Meung [her brother] and me. They didn't have much, but they were willing to share with others. Their generosity turned rainy days into picnics."

These cross-cultural friendships and exchanges reflected the mosaic of people and customs throughout the West. Just as the land was a patchwork of different geographical features, the mixture and interaction of different cultures and ethnic groups stitched together the colorful human quilt of western settlement. Beneath the azure skies of Kansas and the Dakotas, in the shadows of the towering Rockies and down in the dry, brittle canyonlands of New Mexico, on the rolling farmlands of California, Oregon, and Washington, women and men from all walks of life and from across the globe tried to wrest their livelihood from the land—first, as nomadic hunters and gatherers, tillers of the soil and warriors, then as farmers, ranchers, miners, homemakers, and in a myriad of other occupations.

Both native and homesteading women faced new challenges and hardships. As a massive influx of settlers invaded their land, native women struggled to preserve a way of life that had sustained them and their communities. Homesteading women faced different challenges as they strove to make a place for themselves in this burgeoning land. They discovered new skills and inner resources in making their homes, found new ways to earn a living, and eagerly organized reform groups to bring about a better way of life for themselves and their communities. Immigrant and ethnic women faced still different struggles. Women from other countries had to learn a foreign language—English—and adjust to a strange new culture. And, like western women of African and Mexican descent, they bore the cruel bigotry of their white neighbors.

Some women never adjusted to the loneliness or hardships. But other women gradually found a kind of poetry in their natural surroundings. They marveled at the limpid light, the fragrant, colorful wildflowers that grew around their shacks or cabins, the spectacular views and vistas from nearby mountain ranges. Indeed, some women found their greatest refuge in nature. Ruth Flowers and other African-American residents of Boulder, Colorado, learned how to make their own entertainment by hosting ice cream socials and sing-alongs in each other's homes because they were not allowed into restaurants, movie theaters, and other places of recreation in Boulder. But there was one other place where they did not feel shunned or despised, said Ruth, where they were free to go as they pleased: "We hiked in every canyon, and every part of the hills.... The mountains were free and we loved them."

F U R T H E R
R E A D I N G

Diaries, Memoirs, and Letters by Western Women

Alderson, Nannie T., and Helena Huntington Smith. *A Bride Goes West.* Lincoln: University of Nebraska Press, 1969.

Arnold, Mary Ellicott, and Mabel Reed. *In the Land of the Grasshopper Song: Two Women in the Klamath River Indian Country in 1908–09.* Lincoln: University of Nebraska Press, 1980.

Bataille, Gretchen M., and Kathleen Mullen Sands, ed. *American Indian Women: Telling Their Lives.* Lincoln: University of Nebraska Press, 1984.

Calof, Rachel Bella. *Rachel Calof's Story: Jewish Homesteader on the Northern Plains.* Edited by J. Sanford Rikoon. Bloomington: Indiana University Press, 1995.

Cleaveland, Agnes Morley. *No Life for a Lady.* Lincoln: University of Nebraska Press, 1977.

Coker, Caleb, ed. *The News from Brownsville: Helen Chapman's Letters from the Texas Military Frontier.* Austin: Texas State Historical Society, 1992.

Eastman, Elaine Goodale. *Sister to the Sioux: The Memoirs of Elaine Goodale Eastman, 1885–91.* Edited by Kay Graber. Lincoln: University of Nebraska Press: 1978.

Ellsworth, Maria S., ed. *Mormon Odyssey: The Story of Ida Hunt Udall, Plural Wife.* Urbana: University of Illinois Press, 1992.

Fairbanks, Carol, ed. *Writings of Farm Women: An Anthology.* New York: Garland, 1990.

Fischer, Christiane, ed. *Let Them Speak for Themselves: Women in the American West, 1849–1900.* Hamden, Conn.: Archon Books, 1977.

Hafen, Mary Ann. *Recollections of a Handcart Pioneer of 1860: A Woman's Life on the Mormon Frontier.* Lincoln, Nebr.: Bison Books, 1983.

Hampstead, Elizabeth, ed. *Read This Only to Yourself: The Private Writings of Midwestern Women, 1880–1910.* Bloomington: Indiana University Press, 1985.

Hansen, Jennifer M., ed. *Letters of Catharine Cottam Romney, Plural Wife.* Urbana: University of Illinois Press, 1992.

Holmes, Kenneth L., ed. *Covered Wagon Women: Diaries and Letters from the Western Trails, 1840–1849.* Lincoln: University of Nebraska Press, 1995.

Hopkins, Sarah Winnemucca. *Life Among the Piutes.* 1883. Reprint, Reno: University of Nevada Press, 1994.

Hubalek, Linda K. *Butter in the Well: A Scandinavian Woman's Tale of Life on the Prairie.* Hillsboro, Kan.: Hearth Publications, 1992.

Jackson, Helen Hunt. *A Century of Dishonor.* 1881. Reprint, Williamstown, Mass.: Corner House Publishers, 1973.

Jones-Eddy, Julie. *Homesteading Women: An Oral History of Colorado, 1890–1950.* New York: Twayne, 1992.

Kaufman, Polly W., ed. *Apron Full of Gold: The Letters of Mary Jane Megquier from San Francisco, 1849–1856.* Albuquerque: University of New Mexico Press, 1994.

Kohl, Edith Eudora. *Land of the Burnt Thigh.* 1938. Reprint, St. Paul, Minn.: Borealis Books, 1986.

Koren, Elisabeth. *The Diary of Elisabeth Koren.* Translated and edited by David T. Nelson. Northfield, Minn.: Norwegian-American Historical Society, 1955.

Lecompte, Janet. *Emily: The Diary of a Hard-Worked Woman.* Lincoln: University of Nebraska Press, 1987.

Lee, Mabel Barbee. *Cripple Creek Days.* Lincoln, Nebr.: Bison Books, 1984.

Lee, Mary Paik. *Quiet Odyssey: A Pioneer Korean Woman in America.* Edited by Sucheng Chan. Seattle: University of Washington Press, 1990.

Luchetti, Cathy, ed. *Women of the West.* St. George, Utah: Antelope Island Press, 1982.

Lurie, Nancy Oestreich, ed. *Mountain Wolf Woman.* Ann Arbor: University of Michigan Press, 1961.

Miller, Jay, ed. *Mourning Dove: A Salishan Autobiography.* Lincoln: University of Nebraska Press, 1990.

Moynihan, Ruth B., Susan Armitage, and Christiane Fischer Dichamp, eds. *So Much To Be Done: Women Settlers on the Mining and Ranching Frontier.* Lincoln: University of Nebraska Press, 1990.

Niederman, Sharon, ed. *A Quilt of Words: Women's Diaries, Letters & Original Accounts of Life in the Southwest, 1860–1960.* Boulder, Colo.: Johnson Books, 1988.

Qoyawayma, Polingaysi. *No Turning Back: A Hopi Indian Woman's Struggle to Live in Two Worlds.* Albuquerque: University of New Mexico Press, 1977.

Schlissel, Lillian. *Women's Diaries of the Westward Journey.* New York: Schocken Books, 1982.

Stewart, Elinore Pruitt. *Letters of a Woman Homesteader.* 1913. Reprint, Boston: Houghton Mifflin, 1982.

Stratton, Joanna L. *Pioneer Women: Voices from the Kansas Frontier.* New York: Simon & Schuster, 1981.

Thompson, Lucy. *To the American Indian: Reminiscences of a Yurok Woman.* 1916. Reprint, Berkeley, Calif.: Heyday Books, 1991.

Trupin, Sophie. *Dakota Diaspora: Memoirs of a Jewish Homesteader.* Lincoln, Nebr.: Bison Books, 1988.

Underhill, Ruth M., ed. *Papago Woman.* Prospect Heights, Ill.: Waveland Press, 1985.

Viele, Teresa Griffin. *Following the Drum: A Glimpse of Frontier Life.* Lincoln, Nebr.: Bison Books, 1984.

Wilder, Laura Ingalls. *West from Home: Letters of Laura Ingalls Wilder to Almanzo Wilder.* 1915. Reprint, New York: HarperCollins, 1974.

Wilson, Gilbert L., ed. *Waheenee: An Indian Girl's Story.* Lincoln: University of Nebraska Press, 1981.

Histories of Women in the American West

Albers, Annie, and Beatrice Medicine. *The Hidden Half: Studies of Plains Indian Women.* Washington, D.C.: University Press of America, 1983.

Armitage, Sue, Theresa Banfield, and Sarah Jacobus. "Black Women and Their Communities in Colorado," *Frontiers* 2, no. 2 (Summer 1977): 36-40.

Armitage, Sue, and Elizabeth Jameson, eds. *The Women's West.* Norman: University of Oklahoma Press, 1987.

Bahr, Diana M. *From Mission to Metropolis: Cupeneo Indian Women in Los Angeles.* Norman: University of Oklahoma Press, 1993.

Bennion, Sherilyn Cox. *Equal to the Occasion: Women Editors of the Nineteenth-Century Frontier.* Reno: University of Nevada Press, 1990.

Boyer, Ruth M., and Narcissus D. Gayton. *Apache Mothers and Daughters: Four Generations of a Family.* Norman: University of Oklahoma Press, 1992.

Demos, John. *The Tried and the True: Native American Women Confronting Colonization.* New York: Oxford University Press, 1995.

Deutsch, Sarah. *No Separate Refuge: Culture, Class, and Gender on an Anglo-Hispanic Frontier in the American Southwest, 1880–1940.* New York: Oxford University Press, 1987.

Downs, Fane, and Nancy Baker Jones, eds. *Women and Texas History.* Austin: Texas State Historical Society, 1993.

Foote, Cheryl. *Women of the New Mexico Frontier, 1846–1912.* Boulder: University Press of Colorado, 1995.

Frisbie, Charlotte J. *Kinalda: A Study of the Navaho Girl's Puberty Ceremony.* Salt Lake City: University of Utah Press, 1993.

Garcia, Mario T. *Desert Immigrants: The Mexicans of El Paso, 1880–1920.* New Haven: Yale University Press, 1981.

Godfrey, Kenneth W., Audrey M. Godfrey, and Jill Mulvay Derr. *Women's Voices: An Untold History of the Latter-day Saints.* Salt Lake City: Deseret Book Company, 1983.

Goldman, Miriam. *Gold Diggers and Silver Miners.* Ann Arbor: University of Michigan Press, 1981.

Gould, Florence C., and Patricia N. Pando. *Claiming Their Land: Women Homesteaders in Texas.* El Paso: Texas Western Press, 1991.

Gutierrez, Ramon A. *When Jesus Came, the Corn Mothers Went Away: Marriage, Sexuality, and Power in New Mexico, 1500–1846.* Stanford, Calif.: Stanford University Press, 1991.

Harris, Katherine. *Long Vistas: Women and Families on Colorado Homesteads.* Boulder: University Press of Colorado, 1993.

Hurtado, Albert L. *Indian Survival on the California Frontier.* New Haven: Yale University Press, 1988.

Jeffrey, Julie Roy. *Frontier Women: The Trans-Mississippi West, 1840–1880.* New York: Hill and Wang, 1979.

Jensen, Joan M. *One Foot on the Rockies: Women and Creativity in the Modern American West.* Albuquerque: University of New Mexico Press, 1995.

Jensen, Joan M., and Gloria Ricci Lothrop. *California Women: A History.* San Francisco: Boyd & Fraser, 1987.

Jensen, Joan M., and Darlis A. Miller, eds. *New Mexico Women: Intercultural Perspectives.* Albuquerque: University of New Mexico Press, 1986.

Kaufman, Polly Welts. *Women Teachers on the Frontier.* New Haven: Yale University Press, 1984.

LeCompte, Mary Lou. *Cowgirls of the Rodeo.* Urbana: University of Illinois Press, 1995.

Levy, JoAnn. *They Saw the Elephant: Women in the California Gold Rush.* Norman: University of Oklahoma Press, 1992.

Lindgren, H. Elaine. *Land in Her Own Name: Women as Homesteaders in North Dakota.* Fargo: North Dakota Institute for Regional Studies, 1991.

Luchetti, Cathy. *Home on the Range: A Culinary History of the American West.* New York: Villard Books, 1995.

Mihesuah, Devon A. *Cultivating the Rosebuds: The Education of Women at the Cherokee Female Seminary, 1851–1909.* Urbana: University of Illinois Press, 1993.

Milner, Clyde A., ed. *The Oxford History of the American West.* New York: Oxford University Press, 1994.

Myres, Sandra L. *Westering Women and the Frontier Experience, 1800–1915.* Albuquerque: University of New Mexico Press, 1982.

Pascoe, Peggy. *Relations of Rescue: The Search for Female Moral Authority in the American West, 1874–1939.* New York: Oxford University Press, 1990.

Patterson-Black, Sheryll. "Women Homesteaders on the Great Plains Frontier," *Frontiers* 1, no. 2 (Spring 1976).

Peavy, Linda S., and Ursula Smith. *Women in Waiting in the Westward Movement.* Norman: University of Oklahoma Press, 1994.

Perdue, Theda. "Cherokee Women and the Trail of Tears," *The Journal of Women's History* I (1989): 14-28.

Peters, Virginia B. *Women of the Earth Lodges: Tribal Life on the Plains.* North Haven, Conn.: Archon Books, 1995.

Peterson, Susan C., and Courtney A. Vaughn-Roberson. *Women with Vision: The Presentation Sisters of South Dakota, 1880–1985.* Champaign: University of Illinois Press, 1988.

Petrik, Paula. *No Step Backward: Women and Family on the Rocky Mountain Mining Frontier, 1865–1900.* Helena: Montana Historical Society Press, 1987.

Riley, Glenda. *Women and Indians on the Frontier, 1825–1915.* Albuquerque: University of New Mexico Press, 1984.

———. *A Place to Grow: Women in the American West.* Arlington Heights, Ill.: Harlan Davidson, 1992.

Robertson, Janet. *The Magnificent Mountain Women: Adventures in the Colorado Rockies.* Lincoln: University of Nebraska Press, 1990.

Rochlin, Harriet, and Fred Rochlin. *Pioneer Jews: A New Life in the Far West.* Boston: Houghton Mifflin, 1984.

Schakel, Sandra. *Social Housekeepers. Women Shaping Public Policy in New Mexico, 1920–1940.* Albuquerque: University of New Mexico Press, 1992.

Schlissel, Lillian. "Mothers and Daughters on the Western Frontier," *Frontiers* 3, no. 2 (Summer 1978).

———. *Far from Home: Families of the Westward Journey.* New York: Schocken, 1989.

Schlissel, Lillian, Vicki L. Ruiz, and Janice Monk, eds. *Western Women: Their Land, Their Lives.* Albuquerque: University of New Mexico Press, 1988.

Trenton, Patricia, ed. *Independent Spirits: Women Painters of the American West, 1890–1945.* Berkeley: University of California Press, 1995.

Winegarten, Ruthe. *Black Texas Women: 150 Years of Trial and Triumph.* Austin: University of Texas Press, 1995.

Yung, Judy. *Chinese Women of America: A Pictorial History.* Seattle: University of Washington Press, 1986.

———. *Unbound Feet: A Social History of Chinese Women in San Francisco.* Berkeley: University of California Press, 1995.

Biographies

Aikman, Duncan. *Calamity Jane and the Lady Wildcats.* 1927. Reprint, Lincoln: University of Nebraska Press, 1987.

Berry, Michael. *Georgia O'Keeffe.* New York: Chelsea House, 1988.

De Mille, Agnes. *Martha: The Life and Work of Martha Graham.* New York: Random House, 1991.

Ferris, Jeri. *Native American Doctor: The Story of Susan La Flesche Picotte.* Minneapolis: Carolrhoda Books, 1991.

Keene, Ann T. *Willa Cather.* New York: Simon & Schuster, 1994.

Kozodoy, Ruth. *Isadora Duncan.* New York: Chelsea House, 1988.

Mackinnan, Janice and Stephen. *Agnes Smedley: The Life and Times of an American Radical.* Berkeley: University of California Press, 1988.

Mark, Joan. *A Stranger in Her Native Land: Alice Fletcher and the American Indians.* Lincoln: University of Nebraska Press, 1988.

Mathes, Valerie Sherer. *Helen Hunt Jackson and Her Indian Reform Legacy.* Austin: University of Texas Press, 1990.

Miller, Sally M. *From Prairie to Prison: The Life of Social Activist Kate Richards O'Hare.* Columbia: University of Missouri Press, 1993.

Moynihan, Ruth. *Rebel for Rights: Abigail Scott Duniway.* New Haven: Yale University Press, 1983.

Riley, Glenda. *The Life and Legacy of Annie Oakley.* Norman: University of Oklahoma Press, 1994.

Stauffer, Helen Winter. *Mari Sandoz: Story Catcher of the Plains.* Lincoln: University of Nebraska Press, 1982.

Fiction

Austin, Mary Hunter. *The Land of Little Rain.* 1903. Reprint, Albuquerque: University of New Mexico Press, 1974.

Cather, Willa. *My Ántonia.* 1918. Reprint, New York: Penguin, 1994.

———. *O Pioneers!.* 1913. Reprint, New York: Penguin, 1994.

———. *The Song of the Lark.* 1915. Reprint, Boston: Houghton Mifflin, 1988.

Jackson, Helen Hunt. *Ramona: A Story.* Boston: Little Brown, 1932; reprint of 1884 ed.

Mourning Dove. *Cogewea: The Half-Blood.* 1927. Reprint, Lincoln: University of Nebraska Press, 1981.

Osborne, Karen. *Between Earth and Sky.* New York: William Morrow, 1996.

Van Leeuwen, Jean. *Bound for Oregon.* New York: Dial, 1994.

INDEX

Page numbers in *italics* refer to illustrations.

Activists, 166-67
Adams, Cecilia, 74, 86
Adams, Elisabeth, 115
Adobe homes, *96*
African-American women
    club movement of, 160-62
    pioneers, 10, 12, 52-54,
        134-35, 156
    prejudice against, 52, 169-
        71
Aguirre, Mary Bernard, 120
All-black communities, 171-
    72
Allen, Elsie, 39
Amador, Martín and Refugia,
    12
Ammons, Edith and Ida, 93-
    94, 107, 108-9, 111, 117,
    136-38
Anderson, Mary, 113
Anderson, Naomi, 171
Angel Island, 64, 65, *67*
Artists, 149-51

Belknap, Kitturah, 101, 116
Blake, Alice, 143-44
Boardinghouse keepers, *131-*
    33
Boyle, Emmett D., *166*
Brinton, Ada Mae, 100, 119
Buffalo Bird Woman, *24*, 27
Buffalo chips, *73-74*
Businesswomen, 130, 134-35,
    136, 146

Calof, Rachel Bella, 62-63, 64,
    94, 96, 98, 119-20, 122-23,
    124
Carpenter, Helen, 74, 78

Carr, Harriet, 104
Carrillo, Matilde, 141
Cashman, Nellie, 132
Cather, Willa, 47-48
Catholic missionaries, 32-34,
    143-44
Cheese making, 116
Child labor laws, 158
Chinese Exclusion Act (1882),
    67
Chinese women pioneers, 62,
    64-67, 98, 114-15, 133,
    140, 158, 168-69
Churches, *154*
Churchill, Caroline N., 167,
    168
Civil War, 13-14, 45
Club movement, 157-62
Community building, 13,
    154-55
Cook, Lu Lee, 124
Corey, Elizabeth, 95
Coronado, Francisco Vásquez
    de, 30
Cortés, Hernán, 36
Cowgirls, *153*
Crazy Horse, 148-49
Crews, Laura, 47
Cummings, Elizabeth, 87

Dancers, 151-52
Davis, William Heath, 34-35
Dawes Act (1887), 172-73
Deadly, Lucy Henderson, 82
Dearfield, Colo., 171-*72*
Diede, Pauline, 120, 122, 124
Doctors, 144-45
Domestic workers, 134
Donation Land Act (1850), 7
Donner, George, 85
Donner Party, 85
Droughts, 109

Dumont, Ella Bird, 83, 97
Duncan, Isadora, 151-52
Duniway, Abigail Scott, 166-
    67

Eastwood, Alice, 145
Electricity, 55
Ellis Island, 64
Exodusters, *53-54*

Farmers, 138, *148. See also*
    Homesteaders
Farmers' Alliance, 162-63
Fashion magazines, *104*
Fisk, Elizabeth, 126
Flowers, Ruth, 170, 177
Foltz, Clara, 146
Frink, Margaret, 52, 75
Frizzell, Lodisa, 69, 73, 86
Frost, Mary Perry, 83
Fulkerath, Abby E., 69

Gaines, Amanda, 124
Godey's Lady's Book, 104
Gold seekers, 12, 44, 50, 51,
    65, 130, 146
Goldthorpe, Lucy, 49, 107-8
Goodell, Anna, 94
Graham, Martha, 152
Grange movement, 162, *163*
Greenwood, Anna Pike, 110-
    11
Guerin, E. J., 138-39
Guidebooks, 56-57, *59*

Hall, Orrin and Ruth, 121
Hand, Julia, 104
Hannah, Esther, 73
Harper, Sybil, *134*
Hartman, Sarah, 98
Harvey, Fred, 135-36
Harvey Girls, 135-36

Haughey, Mary Gates, 141-42
Haun, Catherine, 79, 87, 88
Hayes, Rutherford B., 174
Health care workers, 144-45
Hecox, Margaret, 38
Hedges, Edna, 126
Helm, Mary, 38
Hickman, Willianna, 53-54
Hines, Celinda, 85-86
Hispanic women pioneers, 10, 12
    Anglos' impressions of, 38-39
    and holidays, 120
    homes of, 96, 97
    legal rights of, 37
    of Los Angeles, 36-37
    marriages of, 121
    and Native Americans, 30-32
    prejudice against, 38-39
    professions of, 134
    roles of, 34-35
Hively, Sarah, 97
Hixon, Adrietta, 89
Holidays, 101, 119-20
Holman, Lois, 117
Homestead Act (1862), 45-46
Homesteaders
    birth control of, 123-24
    and child-rearing, 122, 124-26
    chores of, 99, 100
    cooking of, 100-101
    divorces among, 120-21
    friendships among, 175-76
    homes of, 92-99
    and laundering, 101-2
    mental illness among, 110-11
    new skills of, 11, 13, 104-6, 108
    overview of, 10-11, 45-50
    professions of, 12-13
    and sewing, 103-4
    and sickness, 122-23
    socializing among, 112-120
    and violence, 126-27
    and weather, 107-9
Hunt, Nancy, 78

Immigrant women pioneers, 10, 11, 46, 56, 62-64, 66, 94
Ingall, Sarah T., 138
Ironing parties, 116-17

Irvin, Margaret, 77

Jackson, Helen Hunt, 175
Jackson, Oliver T., 171
Jefferson, Thomas, 43
Jewish women pioneers, 62-63, 119-20, 158
Johnson, Gardener, 44-45
Johnson, Lizzie E., 147
Journalists, 146, 167-68, 170

Kasovich, Israel, 64
Kellie, Luna, 162-63
Ketcham, Rebecca, 75, 82-83
King, Sieh King, 168
Kirk, Katherine, 94
Kirkland, Bulah Rust, 147
Knight, Amelia Stewart, 61-62, 79, 81
Korean women immigrants, 67-69, 109-10, 133-34, 176

Labor unionism, 164
Laundresses, 134
Law, Low Shee, 98
Lawyers, 145-46
Lease, Mary E., 162-63
LeGrand, Anne, 156
Likins, Mrs. J. W., 136
Lincoln, Abraham, 45
Literary societies, 157
Louisiana Purchase (1803), 43-44
Lowry, Annie, 174
Ludlow (Colo.) Massacre (1914), 164
Lund, Alice, 102, 116, 155, 176

McKee, Anna, 38
Malick, Abigail, 7-9, 115-16
Manifest Destiny, 14
Marks, Anna Rich, 146
Martin, Fred, 95-96, 120, 125
Mason, Biddy, 138
Matthews, Rena, 111
Maxwell, Martha, 145
Megquier, Mary Jane, 132
Mexican-American War, 12, 34, 44
Migration, westward
    childbirth during, 81-82
    child-rearing during, 75-76, 88-89
    chores during, 74-75, 77-78

clothing worn during, 77
cooking during, 72-74
dangers of, 85-86
death during, 8, 83-86
decision to undertake, 57-58
illness during, 74, 76-77, 83
loneliness of, 80-81
and Native Americans, 82-83
preparation for, 57
river crossings of, 79, 80, 85-86
socializing during, 87-88
weather during, 79
Miner, Agnes, 126-27
Miners, 146, 163-64
Miranda, Lorencita, 155-56
Missionaries, 32-34, 143-44
Mitchell, Cora Belle, 131
Montezuma, 30
Moore, Melissa Genett, 109, 122
Moral reform societies, 157, 159, 169
Morey, Sarah, 138
Mormons, 54-56, 144, 161, 163, 165
Morris, Esther, 165
Mott, Lucretia, 165-66
Murray, Margaret, 97, 103, 107, 118

National American Woman Suffrage Association, 171
National Association of Colored Women, 160-62
National Woman's Alliance, 163
Nautsiti, 17-18
Native American women, 10, 12, 14
    and age-grade societies, 25-26
    and child rearing, 21, 26-28
    and childbirth, 20
    craftwork of, 17, 22-23, 24-25, 31, 150
    creation stories of, 17-18, 20
    death of, 29-30
    elderly, 29
    government removal of, 40-41
    and Hispanic settlers, 30-34

marriages of, 28, 32
and missionaries, 32-34,
143-44
prejudice against, 39, 82-
83, 172-75
and reservations, 172-75
rituals among, 26, 32
roles of 18-19, 21-25, 39-
40
and settler advancement,
39-40, 41
sexual abuse of, 32, 33
Neblett, Lizzie, 124
Neugin, Rebecca, 40-41
Newcomb, Susan E., 114
Newspaperwomen, 136-37
19th Amendment (U.S.
Constitution), 12, 165, 166
Norris, Eunice, 171
Nutting parties, 119

O'Keeffe, Georgia, 149-50
O'Kieffe, Charley, 74
O'Kieffe, Mary, 49
Orpen, Adele, 125-29
Overland Trail, 9, 50-51, 58-
62, 76. See also Migration,
westward
Overton, Sarah M., 171
Owen, Narcissa Chisholm,
150-51
Owens-Bynum, Harriet, 135

Paik, Mary, 68, 69, 109-10,
133-34, 176
Parsons, Lucene, 55
Paul, Matilda Peitzke, 99, 125
Pelton, Agnes, 149
Pengra, Charlotte Stearns, 77
Periwinkle, Pauline, 167-68
Picotte, Susan La Flesche,
144-45, 174
Plagues, 109
Play-parties, 118-19
Pleasant, Mary Ellen, 134
Pole houses, 96-97
Political activism, 162-66
Polygamy, 54-55, 56, 165
Pomeroy, Mary Annetta
Coleman, 98-99
Poor relief societies, 158-59,
162
Populist party, 162-63
Porter, Lavinia, 55, 80-81
Poston, Mrs. William, 110

Poverty, 109-10
Powers, Mary Rockwood, 87
Prairie fires, 108-9
Prejudice, 38-39, 52, 67-68,
82-83, 109, 143-44, 169-
71, 172-75
Pretty Shield, 174
Prostitution, 65-66, 139-40,
159-60, 169

Queen Bee, 167, 168
Quilting bees, 116

Ranchwomen, 129, 147
Reed, Virginia, 85
Reservation resettlement,
172-73
Rose, Hilda, 106, 159

Sal, Josefa, 141
Sandoz, Mari, 148-49
Sanford, Mollie Dorsey, 89,
113
Santa Cruz, Doña Atanacía,
37
Schools, 156-57
Schurz, Carl, 177
Scientists, 145
Seamstresses, 134, 164
Segale, Sister Blandina, 143
Sepúlveda, Doña Vicente, 34-
35
Serra, Junípero, 32
Sessions, Kate, 138
Sharp, John and Cornelia, 57
Skinner, Mrs. Jared, 101
Slavery, 13-14, 44-45, 138
Smith, Effie Vivian, 157
Smith, Ellen, 84-85
Smith, Florence Blake, 46
Smith, Joseph, 54
Smith, Mary Elizabeth, 118
So, Wong Ah, 62
Soddies, 94-95
Stanton, Elizabeth Cady,
164-65
Staples, Mary Pratt, 113-14
Stewart, Elinore Pruitt, 49-
50, 71, 107
Stewart, Helen Marnie, 59,
80
Stewart, John and Jannet, 90-
91
Strobridge, Ida Meecham,
127

Summerhayes, Martha, 122
Sutherland, Sara Isadore,
167-68
Swan, Lucy, 173

Tate, Emma, 78
Tator, Nettie C., 166
Taylor, Lydia, 140
Teachers, 140-43
Teichert, Minerva Kohlhepp,
151
Thompson, Era Bell, 105-6,
127, 175-76
Tibbets, Eliza, 138
Trail of Tears, 40-41

Viele, Teresa, 38-39
Voting rights, 12, 164-67,
171

Waitresses, 135
Warner, Elizabeth Stewart,
90-91
Welcoming committees, 117
Wetherill, Marietta Palmer,
129-30
Whelan, Rosalía Salazar, 105
Whitaker, Gladys Belvie, 49
Wilder, Laura Ingalls, 148
Wilson, Luzena Stanley, 130
Wilson, Margaret Hereford,
57-58, 81
Wiltbank, Effie May Butler,
118, 123
Wing, Amelia Murdock, 100-
101
Wing, May, 164
Winnemucca, Sarah, 41, 174,
175
Writers, 147-49

Yilan, Liu, 158
Young, Brigham, 54, 144
Young, Maud Fuller, 145
Young Women's Christian
Association (YWCA), 168-
69

Zhouyi, Mai, 65

ACKNOWLEDGMENTS

I wish to thank Professor Elizabeth Jameson of the University of New Mexico for her astute reading of the first draft of the manuscript and for her many suggestions; Nancy Toff, editorial director at Oxford University Press, for her enormous patience and enthusiasm for this project, and for her friendship; Paul McCarthy, senior project editor at Oxford University Press, for his thorough professionalism and meticulous work on my manuscript; my father, Leon Sigerman, who eagerly followed my progress and heartily cheered me on; and, as always, Jay, who shared my passion for telling this story. His love and encouragement are the sunbeams that light my way.